# MEN OF DESTINY

D0590028

# MEN OF DESTINY

TERRY VIRGO

KINGSWAY PUBLICATIONS
EASTBOURNE

Copyright © Terry Virgo 1987

First published 1987
Reprinted 1988
Reprinted 1991

All rights reserved.
No part of this publication may be reproduced or
transmitted in any form or by any means, electronic
or mechanical, including photocopy, recording, or any
information storage and retrieval system, without
permission in writing from the publisher.

ISBN 0 86065 561

Unless otherwise indicated, biblical quotations are from
the New American Standard Bible
© The Lockman Foundation 1960, 1962, 1963,
1968, 1971, 1972, 1973

NIV = New International Version, copyright © International
Bible Society 1973, 1978, 1984.
AV = Authorized Version
crown copyright

*Front cover design by Vic Mitchell*

Printed in Great Britain for
KINGSWAY PUBLICATIONS LTD
1 St Anne's Road, Eastbourne, E. Sussex BN21 3UN by
Clays Ltd, St Ives plc.
Typeset by Nuprint Ltd, Harpenden, Herts.

For Ben, Joel, Simon & Timothy

Praying that you will serve the purpose
of God in your generation.

# Acknowledgements

I want to thank John Parsons, Barry Gould and my wife, Wendy, for all their help in reducing pages of sermon material until it began to take the form of a book.

My thanks are also due to Pamela Haworth and Pauline Jarvis for all the hard work involved in typing and retyping pages of manuscript.

My thanks also to all those who have attended the Downs Bible Week, where inspiration was first provided for the development of this material.

# *Contents*

# Introduction

Three very different characters, but all men of destiny—Joseph the dreamer, the timid Gideon and Nehemiah, the power drill and task-master extraordinary!

Each of them encountered God in a transforming way so that their lives took on new meaning. They endured trials and temptations, but also knew the joys of success and fulfilment. As each laid hold of his destiny, he drew others into God's purpose for their generation. Men who meet God and become joyfully enslaved to his will always affect their contemporaries.

Joseph, having endured great hostility and wickedness against himself, eventually emerged secure in his God, tried and proven worthy of his call, and saving his generation. Gideon, out of weakness, became strong by faith and recruited an army of almost reckless believers who thoroughly turned the tide against the enemy. Nehemiah, the people's general, a giver of hope, whose driven urgency and remorseless energy ensured that the seemingly impossible task was completed.

It is my prayer that as you read these pages, the characters will step out, three-dimensional and relevant to our modern world. Their weaknesses and temptations are not concealed, but neither is the grace of God which helped them prevail, sometimes against overwhelming odds.

We are a generation parched for a rediscovery of heroes. How encouraging, therefore, to find that these Old Testament heroes were essentially flesh and blood like us. As frail men, they encountered the sort of temptations that we meet in the twentieth century. We will recognize ourselves and our circumstances in their experiences. Yet they rose above the trends of their age and proved that God is well able to revolutionize situations if we take him seriously and respond obediently to his initiatives.

Often, we gain new insights into spiritual truths if, in addition to studying theology, we follow the dealings God has with his servants. God has revealed himself not only through his words but also by his actions, and the Bible is not only a book about God but essentially about him in relation to man—and some men in particular.

Each of these men had plenty of reason to throw in the towel. They knew what it was to stand alone before they experienced the dizzy heights of success and popularity. Durability characterized them. These were no comic-strip supermen, transformed by fleeting visits to telephone kiosks! They learned the hard way. In an age of instant stardom and press-button success, we need to face up to the challenge of painful preparation for ministry. Faith must be mixed with patience and fortitude.

These three men of destiny experienced the agonies of being misunderstood and misrepresented. They not only had to fulfil their calling and complete their own particular tasks, they also had to withstand the pressures of opposition and keep their attitudes pure and holy, free from self-pity, self-justification or retaliation.

They did not have the insights of Paul's writings to strengthen them in their resolve. Unlike us, they could not read that the mighty apostle knew what it was to be pressed from all sides yet still not be crushed, perplexed but not despairing, persecuted but not forsaken, knocked down but not knocked out (see 2 Cor 4:8–9). As Christians we have all the revelation of the New Testament at our disposal and, as Peter assures us, God has given us 'everything we need for life and godliness through our knowledge of him' (2 Pet 1:3, NIV).

I trust that as you relive these old stories, your knowledge of him will be expanded, thereby strengthening you to fulfil your destiny in this generation.

The studies recorded in this book have their origins in sermons first preached at the Downs Bible Weeks. These annual summer conferences take place at Plumpton Racecourse, situated just north of my home town of Brighton. Each year thousands gather for these great weeks of celebration, worship, praise and teaching. They started in 1979 with about 3,000 attending and have grown through the years to enjoy attendance figures of around 10,000, forcing the one week to become two.

The sermons were first preached, therefore, to large congregations in a huge marquee in the context of great rejoicing and zeal. I pray that as they now reach you in a totally different form and context, they will prove of lasting worth to the body of Christ at large. I feel that it would be of great value to you to read the Bible stories in conjunction with this book.

# JOSEPH

'And he sent a man before them—Joseph, sold as a slave. They bruised his feet with shackles, his neck was put in irons, till what he foretold came to pass, till the word of the Lord proved him true.'
(Ps 105:17–19, NIV).

# I

## *The Favourite Son*

The story of Joseph is unquestionably one of the most beautiful and intriguing stories ever written. It has all the ingredients for great drama; dreams and visions, family feuds involving envy and hatred, passion and lust, scenes of opulence, the squalor of prison and a meteoric rise to power.

Through it all runs the thread of the character central to the entire saga—Joseph, who starts as a naïve boy, displaying a mixture of innocence and arrogance, and ends up as a man refined by testing circumstances but exalted to a position of enormous power and prominence.

Who was this man? Where did he come from? As with all family epics, many twists and turns conspire to produce the cradle of circumstances into which he was born, so it is necessary to look behind the scenes a little and to understand something of the family background.

Joseph was an especially-loved and longed-for child. His father already had ten sons, but Rachel, his mother, was childless, Her distress was made more acute as her sister, Leah, who was Jacob's first wife, produced children with apparently effortless ease and regularity.

Eventually, Rachel's frustration and disappointment drove her to breaking point. She could not cope with

17

passively waiting and hoping any longer. She must act! She must do something! The tension created by her unhappiness was destroying her marriage.

One day she was shouting irrationally at Jacob and he was reacting angrily. In desperation she proposed a plan whereby she could become a mother by proxy. If Bilhah, her maid, became a surrogate mother, Rachel could take the resulting baby as her own. The plan was put into operation and Dan was born.

Ironically, history was repeating itself. Years before, Jacob's grandfather, Abraham, had found himself in the same plight. His barren wife, Sarah, had offered her maid, Hagar, as a substitute and Ishmael had been born. But the arrival of this unfortunate child had had disastrous repercussions, yet, some two generations later, Jacob and Rachel were resorting to the same idea to solve Rachel's childlessness. They appeared not to have learned from Abraham's experience that short-circuiting God's way, while it may have a short-term, quick result, leads inevitably to complications and confusion.

'God has vindicated me!' cried Rachel exultantly when Dan was born. But it was a lie! It was not God's plan and the very name 'Dan', which means 'God has vindicated me,' eventually disappears from the record. Revelation 7 records the final list of all the tribes of Israel, but Dan's name is not among them. Joseph's name is there and that of Manassah, his son. So in the end Joseph had a double portion as was foretold.

God does not need our engineering and manipulating to bring about his purposes. Eventually, Rachel conceived the longed-for child that God had already chosen and planned for, but she had allowed frustration and disappointment to push her into experimenting with alternatives.

It is by faith and patience that we are to inherit God's blessings. Too often churches have plenty of bright ideas about how they can produce spiritual offspring. It can be hard to wait for God. It can be costly to do things his way. Why be thorough and painstaking when you can get quick results by other means? Why implement scriptural principles of foundation-laying and church building when you can import something colourful and appealing which yields quick results?

It can be costly and painful getting the foundations right and building surely and thoroughly while other churches, which seem content with more superficial methods apparently prosper.

We have to ask some questions. What is our main objective? Self-vindication or a child of God's choosing? Something which grows quickly and fades fast, or something which has slow, small beginnings but which ultimately stands strong and secure because it was initiated by God and nurtured in his way?

Let patience have its perfect work among us. God's work, done in God's time and God's way, will produce God's fruit.


## The favourite son

So at last Joseph was born—special to his father because he was the son of his old age and the son of his beloved wife who had won his heart as a young man. How Jacob lavished his love upon Joseph! Perhaps his joy in him blinded him to the antagonism that such blatant favouritism produced in his ten other sons, for he even favoured Joseph with a highly significant gift—a many-coloured coat. Such a coat was not merely ornamental. It was a sign that the birthright was being passed to him. Reuben should have had it, but he was disqualified for committing sexual sin. All the others were passed over and the birthright went to Joseph. No wonder jealousy began to take root in the hearts of the brothers!

Joseph's behaviour added further fuel to the fire of their envy. With the naïve unwariness of a seventeen year old, he reported back to his father some questionable activities which his brothers were indulging in. This so exacerbated their hostility that they could hardly bring themselves to speak to him. But in happy ignorance—or was he just plain obnoxious?—he fanned the flame yet again by recounting a dream that he had had.

In his dream they were binding sheaves of corn in a field when, suddenly, Joseph's sheaf arose and all the brothers' sheaves prostrated themselves around it. Understandably, they were more inflamed at this, and even his father rebuked him when he recounted a dream in which eleven stars and the sun and moon were bowing down to him. Obviously, the boy was getting delusions of grandeur!

Poor Joseph! The visionary, the dreamer, so blessed and excited at being the recipient of such revelation, little realized what antagonism was being stirred up in the hearts of those who had not been granted such revelation.

One day, an unexpected opportunity for revenge arose. Jacob sent Joseph to find his brothers who were tending the flocks way out in the country. They saw him coming and plotted to kill him. However, Reuben managed to restrain them from actual murder and they threw him down a well instead, eventually selling him to a camel train bound for Egypt.

So the extraordinary drama unfolds, containing as much intrigue, jealousy and hatred as a TV soap opera. Yet it has far more significance and purpose than a mere entertaining tale. It is not only the true account of a man's life, for we find woven into it another story told from God's perspective.

Two generations before, God had told Abraham,

> Know for certain that your descendants will be strangers in a land that is not theirs, where they will be enslaved and oppressed four hundred years...afterward, they will come out with many possessions...in the fourth generation they shall return here (Gen 15:13–16).

Joseph was a key part of a plan that was far broader in its scope than one man's life. And yet the details of that life were so important to the success of that plan. A sovereign God was unfolding his divine purposes that would reach down the ages. His plan for the nation of Israel hinged upon the life of this young man. God needed a man whom he could trust in a position of enormous power. That man, therefore, had to be utterly impervious to charm and flattery, not given to being vindictive, free from hidden guilt, a man who had proved himself reliable, hard-working and efficient, skilled in administration, wise and compassionate.

Where would he find such a paragon? He would select a man before he was born, place him in a certain family environment and put him through a rigorous training programme. Joseph's reactions to the apparently random and cruel events that he suffered and his demeanour during them were crucial to the success of the plan as a whole. Behind the scenes, God was at work.

Jesus' words, 'What I do now you know not, but afterwards you will understand', could have been written over Joseph's life many times. Psalm 105:17 says: 'He sent a man before them, Joseph, who was sold as a slave.' The brothers acted out of envy and spite but the psalmist claims that God was responsible!

# 2

## *Seeing Visions and Dreaming Dreams*

The Bible speaks of a God who reigns over everything. Many, like Joseph, know what it is to be tossed about on the waves of life, but this truth can hold them like an anchor. When circumstances change, sometimes suddenly and dramatically, do we still know who is on the throne? God rules over everything and the way he establishes his rule is not through vague patronage from heaven, but by being involved in the detail of individual lives. That is why, just as Joseph's brothers were plotting to eliminate him, a caravan of nameless Ishmaelite merchants 'happened' to arrive. The timing was perfect. God's plan entered the next phase.

We see the same phenomenon repeatedly in the Bible. The story of Esther is a complicated one, but one detail is crucial: one night the king could not sleep. This seemingly trivial event proved to be pivotal to the nation's history. God even arranged a king's insomnia in order to bring about his plans. God rules over amazing details of timing.

He also rules over mighty nations—over China, India, Russia and the USA. He is King. He lifts up men and puts them down. He closes China and lets communism rampage through the land. He promotes a common language. He uses communism to deal with the challenge of rampant idolatry and then opens the door again. The next thing we hear is that throughout China there are millions of Christians.

So Joseph, who seemed to be going from one catastrophe to another, was actually safe in the hands of Almighty God. He had been chosen by God and was being prepared for a part to play in history. *We also* have been chosen to walk in good works foreordained by God. When that awesome fact grips us, we can take pressure, delay, opposition or hindrance, because Almighty God has laid hold of us and said, 'This is my chosen instrument to accomplish my purposes.'

We are not just a mass of reactions to circumstances. Philosophers, sociologists and psychologists will explain our lives, personalities and characters from the human perspective. But if I am assured that God is over all, I can see things from a divine viewpoint. I can ask with excitement, 'What will God do with my life?' As people of destiny we should, like Paul, make it our ambition to lay hold of that for which God has laid hold of us.


## Visions and dreams

Before continuing to the next intriguing episode in Joseph's story, I want to draw your attention to something about Joseph's experience that has a familiar New Testament ring to it. Perhaps you have noticed a phrase being used that is reminiscent of a quotation in the book of Acts. Here was a man who saw visions and dreamed dreams!

Tragically, as he recounted them to his brothers they turned against him and threw him out. But as he submitted to the pressures of God's training programme, he became a strong and mature man who ultimately led his brothers into blessing. His visions were vindicated. His family was saved from disaster and so was the whole of Egypt.

Here I believe we have a picture not unlike what is happening today. God promised in the prophecy of Joel that he would pour out his Spirit on all people, and that young and old would see visions and dream dreams. Many Christians world-wide have been freshly filled with the Holy Spirit and have started experiencing supernatural gifts. But often, as they have tried to share their testimony, they have not been well received. Perhaps they have been insensitive in the way they have shared it. Perhaps they plunged in unwisely and seemed to present a threat rather than the promise of more abundant life. But it is sadly true that many people have found sharing the vision has resulted in rejection of both them and their message.

Sometimes Christians have been chagrined, even offended, when someone whom they regarded as an up-start, maybe even a 'younger brother', claims to have had experiences of the Holy Spirit. They cannot take him seriously! They wrote him off years ago! Yet there he is having visions and prophecies and getting altogether too much of the limelight. Who does he think he is?

It is tragic when Christians respond so negatively to the blessing of another Christian. Joseph's brothers were not the only ones to react this way. When David, young and brave, boldly strode into the Israelite camp one day and offered to meet Goliath's challenge, his big brothers were shocked and offended at what they regarded as sheer presumption.

Joseph may have been a green young man, full of himself, irritating in his self-assurance, but he was speaking the truth. He *had* seen a vision! Tragically, some people, when hearing the testimony of another, read into that testimony an implied comment on themselves.

'So you see visions, do you?'

'So you've received the Holy Spirit and speak in tongues, do you?'

'So you're saying that you have something that I don't have, are you? You're making out that you're better than I am, aren't you? You are implying that I'm some sort of second-class Christian.'

Tragically, people leap to conclusions, get defensive, hostile and bitter.

One Christian wrote a book in which he sarcastically described Christians in charismatic churches as 'the charismatic super-sainthood movement'. Tension is brought to God's family as Christians react against each other. It has become very difficult to share testimony honestly without being misunderstood.

There is a wonderful story told in the Old Testament about four lepers outside the city of Samaria which was in the throes of a siege; famine was raging. The lepers decided that as they were going to die anyway they might as well cast themselves on the enemy. They had nothing to lose.

They went down to the enemy camp and were amazed to find it totally deserted. The enemy had unaccountably fled. They discovered tent after tent full of food, clothes and riches! Jubilantly they exclaimed, 'This is not a day to keep silence! Let's go and tell the city!' They were only lepers, but they had stumbled on something which had to be shared!

They returned to the city, and the initial response to their news was suspicion, but eventually the king was persuaded to send out a search party to investigate. The lepers' story was confirmed and the starving Samaritans rushed out and plundered the camp.

There are many Christians today who feel starved. They are despondent and besieged by hosts of enemy doubts and fears. Then comes news of abundance! The miracle-working God does not belong to some past dispensation! He is even now at work and wants to bless them too. The messengers may be less than perfect—even a bit uncouth—but the message is genuine! The food is there! The only barriers are cynicism and unbelief.

When Joseph shared his testimony he was rejected. The temptation to keep quiet about blessings received can be very great as no one enjoys rejection. But truth and honesty were at stake. Did Joseph have a genuine vision or not?

Today some, like Joseph, are being prepared for future ministry. As time goes on, foundational ministries such as apostles and prophets will emerge. Will there be an enthusiastic and happy response? There will be from some. From others, inevitably, there will be cynical remarks and rumours.

'Have you heard? So-and-so claims to be an apostle.'

'Really? Thinks he can rival St Paul, does he?'

'Worse! Probably claims infallibility!'

'Well, we can't possibly go along with that heretical nonsense!'

'Of course, God exalts the humble. He can't possibly bless such presumption. It can't be of God.'

As men honestly seek to rediscover the teaching of the New Testament and the place of the ministries listed in Ephesians 4, there will be a strong temptation to dilute our terminology with more palatable words. We could say that someone 'gives counsel' into a church or is 'helping it to develop'. We could talk about people 'having something of an apostolic function', rather than call them apostles outright, in an attempt to make it sound more acceptable. But if we do we shall lose our edge, then we shall lose our vision and finally we will lose our way. We must be honest and true to our vision, though we may have to pay the same price that Joseph paid in terms of rejection.

It is the responsibility of those who see visions and dream dreams to be true to their vision. They must also continually seek God's help to put no unnecessary stumbling block before their brothers through unwarranted arrogance. May God help us all as we seek to go forward to fulfil his purpose in our generation.

# 3

## A Successful Man

He could have protested, 'I was only true to my vision. I only shared what God had shown me! Now look at me—separated from my parents, my brothers, far from home in another country, a slave with no rights and no future. It's all so unjust!' He could have been devastated by that one experience but, amazingly, we read that there in Egypt Joseph *became a successful man*. Although his circumstances were so grim, he prospered because God was with him.

What could that tell me about Joseph? First, it tells me that he refused to live in the past. He flatly rejected the temptation to harbour resentment about what his brothers had done to him. He was not found wallowing in self-pity. Many people have their whole lives spoilt because they carry hurts and grudges about past events. They remember the way someone spoke to them, the way they were treated, sometimes years ago. Many people nurse an ugly root of bitterness and then wonder why their lives bear little fruit. They long to pray, be filled with the Spirit and be fed by the Bible, but inwardly they smoulder with a bitterness that spoils the work of grace in their lives.

I wonder if you are tempted to mutter to yourself, 'If only that had not happened, all would have been well'; 'If only they had not treated me like that, I would be on course'; 'It's not my fault that I'm not making progress.' Often, we make excuses for ourselves while bitterness festers within and distorts our growth. Many ask, 'Lord, why did you let this happen to me?' We want God to explain everything to us, but Bible characters often went through all kinds of pressures which were left unexplained. They had to learn to leave things with God.

You might be smarting from unexpected heartaches, broken engagements, illnesses, bereavement or loss. Any of these could give rise to resentment and bitterness. Perhaps you are resentful towards someone, or a group of people, who have distorted your testimony. Receiving the baptism of the Holy Spirit was perhaps one of the happiest experiences of your life, but went on to lead to angry accusations against you that escalated into a furious row, terminating with your being asked to leave. You may be seething with bitterness at what you regard as cruel and unjust treatment. But you must determine to leave the past behind and walk away free.

If you carry in your spirit things against God or against your brothers or sisters, you will never experience all that God has for you, however much you apply yourself to other things such as prayer, Bible reading or trying to become free in worship. You will never be recorded as 'a successful man', or 'a prosperous woman', because that root of bitterness will spoil everything. Joseph had plenty of reasons to be sour, but he rejected them.

### Forgive and forget

We must break free by a deliberate decision! As children of God we deliberately decide to forgive because God has given us grace to do so. God has shown mercy to us sinners and thereby provided us with powerful motivation for forgiving others. To encourage us, Jesus spoke some awesome words: 'If you forgive men for their transgressions, your heavenly Father will also forgive you. But if you do not forgive men, then your heavenly Father will not forgive your transgressions' (Mt 16:14–15). Jesus taught us a prayer which contains these lines, 'Forgive us our trespasses as we forgive those who trespass against us.' In other words we are saying, 'Forgive me, Lord, in the way that I forgive others.' If we are not giving away forgiveness, we are not going to receive any ourselves. Will you maintain the discipline of praying that prayer regularly? Can you ask for forgiveness, secure in knowing you will receive it because you have a forgiving spirit yourself?

Decide to live like that! You can do it. Do not say, 'I'm only human.' You are not 'only human'. You are one who has found grace in the eyes of the Lord. You have been forgiven much! Jesus taught quite clearly and plainly that for a believer to cling to a resentment towards someone else is an outrage before him. He told a parable about a man who was forgiven a vast debt and then demanded repayment of a very small amount owing to him. When this man's refusal to forgive was discovered by the one who had released him from his great debt, he was outraged! How could he insist on repayment of such a petty claim, when he had been let off so much himself?

Jesus made it very plain that we do not need some special touch from God to be set free to forgive. We do not need to seek prayer from a preacher or special ministry. We forgive because we are children of God and the Spirit of Christ is in us. If there is one thing that Christians should excel at it is forgiving other people.

## Walk by faith

Not only did Joseph forgive and forget the past, he also steadfastly maintained a stance of faith. His testimony is one of the outstanding illustrations that God makes all things work together for good to those who love him and

are called according to his purpose. Living long before
Romans 8:28 was penned, Joseph seemed to have the
truth written on his heart. It is one of the great promises
that should make Christians shine in a world where people
are tormented by fear and anxiety. When we are assured
of God's overruling providence, we can live with poise
and praise. The fact that everything is working together
for good becomes a well of water springing up in our
spirit. Having confidence that God is on the throne is what
changes and transforms us. Having forgiven and forgotten, we maintain our joy and peace by believing God,
and in this way we become lights in the world.

In Philippians 2:14–15 Paul tells us as Christians,

> Do all things without grumbling or disputing; that you may
> prove yourselves to be blameless and innocent, children of
> God above reproach in the midst of a crooked and perverse
> generation, among whom you appear as lights in the world.

Often we wonder how to shine as a light in the world.
Here is one way that is very clear. We are in the midst of a
world that complains all the time. The world seems sadly
to complain about any situation. If it has been a fine week
we often hear the complaint that it is bound to rain
because the weekend is coming! People complain about
the buses always being late, about the way the office is
run, about the school, about the management, about the
men. We constantly hear this dull, grating noise of complaint and ingratitude.

The church shines as a light in the world, not only by
proclaiming Jesus in the streets but also by doing all things
without grumbling and complaining. That is enough to
make you shine today! Remember to keep shining! Exhort
one another all the time—husbands, wives, parents of
Christian children—we must stop one another in our
tracks and say, 'Remember you're a Christian.

Remember to do all things without grumbling and complaining!'

That proves we are 'children of God without reproach'. Joseph was like that and it made him stand out. He had learned to give thanks in everything and not complain.

There are two languages in the world—the language of complaint and the language of thanksgiving, and there are some who live on the borderland and speak both languages. Don't live on the border learning that foreign language. Be a true native of Zion!

## Beware the dim, distant future

Joseph was not dwelling in the past, but neither was he living in the future in a haze of dreams and fantasies. The fact that Joseph was a successful man is clear proof that he was not projecting everything into the future. How easily he could have been dominated by the thought 'one day I'll get out of here'.

Projecting everything into the future, we can fail to apply God's grace in the present so we are for ever living in frustration and unfulfilment. It is so easy to live in a world of unreality. 'When I get away from home and leave my unbelieving family, then I can mix with other Christians and be a real testimony.' Then, at university, we can argue, 'I must get my degree first. When I've finished at university, I'll really live for God.' Having met Mister or Miss Right, we can think that once we are married and have our own Christian home we will shine for God.

So often we chafe at the restrictions of the moment and use them as an excuse for not bearing fruit. We can dream that sometime in the future God will begin to move mightily by his Spirit and we shall do great exploits, but everything is in the distant, misty future in a life supposedly free from present complications and limitations. Some argue that they know they have received a call and when they become full time it will change every-

thing. But Joseph bore fruit while he was in the house of
his master, the Egyptian. In spite of all the restrictions, he
was a successful man and the Lord even blessed Potiphar's
house because of him. Eventually Potiphar gave him more
responsibility so that the Lord blessed all that he owned
on account of Joseph.

## Kingdom principles

In Luke 16:10–12, Jesus laid down some definite kingdom
principles, saying,

> He who is faithful in a very little thing is faithful also in much;
> and he who is unrighteous in a very little thing is unrighteous
> also in much. If therefore you have not been faithful in the use
> of unrighteous mammon, who will entrust the true riches to
> you? And if you have not been faithful in the use of that which
> is another's, who will give you that which is your own?

Here we see three statements which Jesus gave as laws
of the kingdom which must affect our way of life. We have
to be faithful in the little things. Joseph was not found
murmuring, 'I suppose I'd better serve in this awful place.
One day, when I get out, they'll see what I'm made of.
One day they're going to bow to me, one day.... Meanwhile I have to look after this God-forsaken hole that is
not worthy of me.' Do we find Joseph murmuring with
resentment? No. He brought blessing to his master's
house! As we tackle our present responsibilities faithfully
God takes note!

God is looking for those who are faithful in the use of
'unrighteous mammon', such as money, possessions,
houses—in fact, everyday commodities that are part of
everyday life. We can make false distinctions between
what is 'of the world' and what is 'of the kingdom', then all
those things with a 'mammon' label we relegate to the
secular or regard as worldly. The next step is to say,

'These things do not pertain to the kingdom so it does not matter how I treat them.' The temptation quickly follows to be less than thorough at work, to rush off quickly to attend meetings leaving things undone, or to be inefficient in the name of 'putting first the kingdom of God'. God, however, is looking for diligence and righteousness while we are dealing with 'mammon'.

Joseph's experience in Potiphar's house was all part of his training for the ministry that lay ahead of him. God is now looking upon many a life and asking, 'Does this one qualify to have authority in my church? Can he or she cope with the full glare of publicity? Can his life stand up to scrutiny? Has he already proved himself honourable in small details when no one was watching except me?' Are you faithful at work? Do you do a good job or do you think, 'I can't wait to get away from this awful place.' God forewarns us, 'If you have not been faithful in the use of that which is another's, who will give you your own?' David looked after a few sheep which were not his own but his father's, yet he did it so meticulously, so carefully, so responsibly, that God lifted him from shepherding a few sheep and said, 'Now you shepherd my nation!'

Joseph was faithful though a slave in a foreign land. As we rejoice in the rediscovery of spiritual gifts and charismatic worship, we are not to fool ourselves that God is no longer interested in character development. He monitors our reactions to see whether we are ready for true riches; whether we can have what is our own.

I am sure that he watches over the way we have cared for our small house group—those twelve people who come every week. God would say, 'I have watched over the way you have cared for your little flock and not deplored the fact that you are not speaking to hundreds. I have watched your faithfulness.' God watches us just as he watched over Joseph.

Joseph was not preoccupied with looking back, nor was he only dreaming of the future. He was living in the present and using it as a training programme. Joseph was running the race and running it well, but into his world, suddenly, came another fearful challenge.

# 4

## *'Lie with Me'*

We do not live in a spiritually neutral environment. We live in a world where Satan has many ways of attacking and undermining. He can assume many different disguises to trick us and discredit the work of God. As we read on in this story, so relevant to the days in which we live, Potiphar's wife appears on the scene. Here is Joseph—away from home and its restrictions—young and handsome and beginning to make his mark. His outstanding success makes him even more attractive. Now Potiphar's wife begins to turn her eye upon him. Her husband is often away from home. She is alone, available and willing. Powerful temptation suddenly stares this young man in the face.

This probably attractive woman who had power and authority found him desirable and wanted him for herself. The challenge was sudden and outrageous. Suddenly, and quite openly, she invited him to lie with her, and this young man found himself encountering a situation he had never faced before. Without warning, an unexpected road to fulfilment opened before him—alluring, fascinating, begging to be explored. Temptation is often like that—sudden, with the promise of instant satisfaction. That is why it is so powerful. 'I can satisfy you now, immediately,' it whispers urgently. It can ruin a whole life in a moment of time.

Earlier in the Old Testament we find Esau stumbling in from the fields, famished. He smells the inviting aroma of meat which Jacob is cooking and blurts out, 'Give me some of that red stew' (see Genesis 25:30). His flesh was crying out for fulfilment; its demand overriding his spirit. 'I want to be satisfied and I want it now!' That expression of Esau's so sums up the longings of the flesh. When Jacob replied that it would cost him his inheritance, he answered that he cared nothing about his inheritance. 'Give me some of that red stew now!' Temptation has the ability to make all that is spiritual and godly fade from view while the flesh clamours for immediate satisfaction. For Esau, a massive tug-of-war began as this young man was invited to forfeit his inheritance and indulge his appetite. He failed miserably.

Today young people leave home, go away to college, to university or even on a holiday. They find that temptations they have never faced before are suddenly upon them with ferocious intensity. It is all so easy now—it is all so possible. The restrictions have disappeared. Suddenly, temptation can be overwhelming.

For Joseph, not only was it sudden, it was sustained. Genesis tells us that she entreated him 'day after day' (39:10). Day after day! You wonder how Joseph maintained his purity. He was not like Samson who withstood at first, but when pressed day after day, yielded. Sometimes we face prolonged periods of temptation.

Not only was it sustained, it was subtle. Genesis continues, 'He did not listen to her to lie beside her, or be with her' (v.10). In other words, there was an alternative; he would not actually go to bed with her and lie with her, but couldn't he just spend some time with her, perhaps indulge in a little harmless flirtation, seeing just how far they could go? People often think they can play with fire and remain unburned. They do not intend to be totally, irrevocably committed to adultery, but they cannot bring themselves to be drastic and final either. So they indulge in a little intrigue. But before they retreat, the flirtation has been fanned into a fire. This subtle alternative confronted Joseph.

Then Satan played another ace. Joseph knew that Potiphar's wife had authority through her husband. 'Perhaps she could get me out of this situation. If I went along with her, perhaps she could pull some strings to get me out of this whole predicament.' Surely Satan underlined Joseph's awful sense of being unloved and lonely and away from home. Other people did not love him and now, suddenly, this woman desired him. She was showing him attention if no one else was. The powerful subtlety of it all! Satan whispered his insidious arguments relentlessly, pressurizing him to throw away his purity.

### No one can see

Not only was this attack sudden, sustained and subtle, it was also secret. She said, 'There is no one else here. No one else will know about it—just you and me. No one needs to know. No one can see what is happening here in the dark between us.' The truth of the matter is that all heaven was looking on. All heaven was watching this young man called by God in the midst of great pressures and difficulties. He was in the centre of God's will, set fair for a glorious future fulfilling the purpose of God. Today we might think there is no one looking at us, but in fact all heaven is looking on and wondering, 'Will this young man or woman triumph, or will they throw everything away in one moment of foolishness?'

So often the devil tells us lies like: 'No one can see.' We forget that God is with us all the time and we cannot hide from him. Everything is open to him. He observes our response on the evil day. It is no good saying, 'My New Year's resolution is that I will not be tempted this year.' There will *always* be temptation. Even Jesus was tempted! In Deuteronomy 8:2 it says: 'God has led you in the wilderness these forty years...to know what was in your heart.' He allows us to be in situations that reveal our inner motivations. His aim is to make us like Jesus, who loved righteousness and hated iniquity.

How did Joseph overcome? First of all, he overcame by being the very opposite to Eve in the garden. God had said to Eve, 'You may eat of any of the trees except one.' But because she had already become preoccupied with that other tree when the devil approached her, she was open to temptation. Joseph's attitude was completely different. When Potiphar's wife spoke to him he replied, 'Your husband has given me everything else except you because you are his wife.' His attitude was unlike Eve's. She had already forgotten the other trees, and longed only for the fruit of *that* tree.

In contrast, Joseph said, 'I thank God that he has given me everything else. It is only right that he should withhold you.' I believe that his reply was rooted in the attitude we noted earlier, namely, that he received all things without grumbling or complaining. He was enjoying all that God had already given. He had a positive attitude, a clear perspective to his life.

If our whole attitude to life is essentially one of thanksgiving and praise and acceptance of all that God has given, when some other thing is offered to us we are already fulfilled, having already accepted from God what he has graciously given. This is to be our basic attitude to life. People who are bitter, who feel that things are not all that they should be, who complain 'nobody loves me', are far more vulnerable to this kind of temptation because they are always longing for something different in which to find fulfilment.

## Call a spade a spade

Joseph had another weapon whereby he was enabled to overcome temptation. He did not hesitate to name what she offered as 'evil'. He replied, 'Why should I do this great evil?' He was under no illusions about that. We must start calling a spade a spade. The world tries to deceive us by cunningly changing the terminology. It speaks of 'free love' and the resulting children as 'love children'. It wants to talk about 'indiscretions'. The terminology has changed so that sin has become acceptable. Sin is no longer regarded as sin if it is 'meaningful'. Sexual experimentation is only wrong today if people do not 'love' one another. We hear so often, 'We love each other, don't we? That's all that matters.'

Across our nation there are vast numbers of charismatic young people who see visions and dream dreams—young people and even children who are entering into a new spiritual dimension, who are living in the midst of a crooked and perverse generation, a generation that says, 'Come, lie with us.' It is the accepted thing. 'Everyone else is doing it, so why should you be the only girl in the class who has kept herself clean?' Siren voices beckon, 'Come lie with us, come and be like us. Why do you hold on to those old-fashioned ways?' Joseph overcame by being very clear about the issues. We have to be equally as clear and say, 'To do such-and-such is a great evil.' It is not just 'free love'. It is not just 'meaningful'. It is a great evil!

We need to wake up to the fact that compromise abounds in all areas of life, not simply in sexual sin. The stealing that takes place at work, the shoplifting, the tax fiddles, are all regarded as common-place and growingly acceptable. There are major companies today that build into their accounts a percentage to compensate for the amount that will be stolen from them by their employees, taken away from the factory in pockets, in the boots of cars and on the backs of lorries. It is a way of life now. Everybody does it.

In sport we find the 'professional foul', which is really cheating, spoils and robs us of the joys of true sport. The moral fibre of our nation is being whittled away as the world invites us, 'Come lie with us.' Why do you have to be so different? Behind it all is the devil with his antagonism, all his passion to spoil. Joseph called it a great evil. He called it what it was and saw that it was against God: 'Why should I do this great evil and sin against God?' A generation that is losing all its signposts is a nation that has forgotten that sin is an offence against God.

'Sin' is a religious word. It is not just that I sin against my brother or my sister and so spoil their lives, but my sin is also against God. In the end, that was what devastated David after he had sinned with Bathsheba. He admitted, 'Against Thee, Thee only I have sinned' (Ps 51:4). He could not escape his crippling guilt.

Joseph, however, was steadfast. Day by day he refused to give in, and maintained his integrity. He could not tell his master. As a slave he could not run away. He was shut in. What was he to do? Finally she forced herself upon him. As she clung to his sleeve, willing him to share her life, he wrenched himself free and fled, leaving her holding his garment. So desperate was he to leave the danger zone. All heaven must have rejoiced. He had come through the test! He was vindicated!

In the film *Chariots of Fire* about two young men who were invited to Paris to race in the 1924 Olympic Games, one of them, a Christian named Eric Liddell, was horrified to find that the heat for the 100-yard race would be run on a Sunday. Pressure was brought to bear upon him by the authorities, but his sustained refusal to run on the Sunday brought the film to a thrilling climax. Finally, he agrees to run in the 400 yards, a distance for which he has not trained. As he is waiting, ready to run the race of a lifetime, someone thrusts into his hand a scrap of paper on which is written: 'Those who honour God, God will honour.' The starting pistol breaks the silence and the 400-yards race is underway. The excitement mounts as this tremendous sprinter thunders round the track clutching in his hand the crumpled promise. And of course he won a famous victory! A friend who saw the film in London told me that at the end the entire cinema audience stood and applauded.

Liddell was lifted shoulder high and carried out triumphant. He had won the race. He had been true to his convictions and was gloriously vindicated. But remember Joseph. He was also true to his convictions, and look what happened to him! His coat was torn from his back; Potiphar's wife screamed that he had molested her. Naturally, her lies were believed and he was thrown into prison, but God had a great redemptive purpose for Joseph.

# 5

## *Promotion to Prison*

Full of integrity, and resisting sin at great cost, Joseph was not carried shoulder high by an exultant throng, but was lied against, ridiculed and thrown into prison. Honouring God does not always result in being acclaimed by the crowd. His integrity cost Joseph everything. But, if we could see this disaster from heaven's perspective, we would see the angels rejoicing over Joseph even as men were casting him into prison. From God's viewpoint, Joseph had triumphed. He was on course, ready for the next stage that would prepare him for God's ultimate purpose in his life.

God carefully, painstakingly, orchestrates the details of our lives. Salvation is free, but preparation for spiritual authority is often costly and difficult.

Joseph was in the furnace, being prepared for future ministry. Psalm 105:19 reminds us that the word of the Lord *refined* him. Elijah knew a similar experience. Hardly had that amazing man arrived on the scene when God directed him to the brook at Cherith to be fed by ravens. Day by hot, dusty day the meagre trickle dwindled in the drought. He must have watched it anxiously. At last God stepped in: 'Elijah, go to Zarephath where I have commanded a widow woman to feed you.' But one thing

God omitted to mention was that the widow woman was starving, nearly at death's door! Having arrived at this hopeless rendezvous, he discovered all kinds of tests awaiting him. While he was there, her only son was going to die. The very name 'Zarephath' means 'the place of refining, the place of the crucible'.

God tries his saints. He puts them into the crucible to refine their lives. When we tell God that we want to serve him with our lives in order to see his kingdom come, he tests us to see if that is what we really want. Often, this testing involves going through a furnace. Often, we are tempted to ask, 'Lord, how much longer is this pressure going to last? I can't understand why it is so prolonged and so difficult.'

Why did Elijah have to go from one pressure to another? Because God had a great plan for Elijah. He was going to stand before the whole nation of Israel and call down fire from heaven, and then open the skies after three years of drought. God painstakingly prepares a man who is going to have a significant ministry.

Recently, I read some of the story of Elvis Presley who leapt from obscurity to international fame overnight. Suddenly it seemed he could rule the world—but at what a price! Very quickly he became dependent on drugs until, in the end, still a young man, his life collapsed in ruins. His sudden rise to fame ruined him.

### Sure foundations

Let me put it another way. Why are foundations laid under a building? I recall some years ago when we endured a terrible furnace experience in our church. God spoke to us in prophecy: 'I know how large the building will be. That is why I am taking such pains over the foundations.' God knows what he wants to build and how significant our testimony is going to be and so he takes time with us. When you question why life is so difficult, God replies,

'What I do you do not realize now, but you shall understand hereafter' (Jn 13:7).

We must take courage from the Scriptures. Encouraged
by them, we can see how the story ends. But God's word
must work its way into our hearts. Psalm 66:10 says:
'Thou hast tried us, O God; Thou hast refined us as silver
is refined. Thou didst bring us into the net.' Who did? The
devil? No, God! '*You* brought us into the net. *You* laid
burdens on our backs. *You* made men ride over our
heads; we went through fire and through water, but *you*
brought us out into a place of abundance.' You can write
'Joseph' against that in your Bible's margin. That is exactly
what he went through and was eventually brought out
'into a place of abundance'.

So often when we go through pressure we wonder if the
devil is oppressing us, but even when evil men seem
responsible they only prove to be God's instruments in a
great plan.

Paul says,

> We do not want you to be unaware, brethren, of our affliction
> which came to us in Asia, that we were burdened excessively,
> beyond our strength, so that we despaired even of life; indeed,
> we had the sentence of death within ourselves in order that we
> should not trust in ourselves, but in God who raises the dead
> (2 Cor 1:8–9).

He continues,

> We have this treasure in earthen vessels, that the surpassing
> greatness of the power may be of God and not from ourselves;
> we are afflicted in every way, but not crushed; perplexed, but
> not despairing; persecuted, but not forsaken; struck down,
> but not destroyed; always carrying about in the body the dying
> of Jesus, that the life of Jesus also may be manifested in our
> body. For we who live are constantly being delivered over to

death for Jesus' sake, that the life of Jesus also may be manifested in our mortal flesh (2 Cor 4:7–11).

What does a furnace do? It burns up rubbish which is not only dirty but unnecessary and extraneous; things that are not worth clinging to; things that take up space, that clutter our lives. So God wants to remove the litter from our lives. He wants us to see what is essential and has lasting value. We are running in a race. We cannot run well if we are hampered by excess baggage.

## Burning the rubbish

In the parable of the sower Jesus said that there are those who immediately respond to the word and then the sun rises. Their swift response is tested. Jesus did not say, 'And then, one day, the sun *might* rise.' The sun has a definite tendency to rise! Our impulsive and oft-times emotional responses are tested.

God not only burns up our emotional responses, he challenges our cold, doctrinal correctness when it is not built on genuine faith! We can be meticulous in defending such doctrines as the sovereignty of God and yet be tense, nervous and defensive because these doctrines have never entered our hearts. No, if we believe these great doctrines then they should build security into our lives—total peace and rest. Those who believe in the sovereignty of God should be like a rock, secure and immovable, not frightened men!

It is better that we find out what we really are through the fire. It delivers us from our self-sufficiency, from thinking we can make it on our own. When we go through the test, we discover how weak and needy we are and realize the danger of being exalted prematurely to a position that we cannot handle. God is preparing his church for end-time prominence when she shall arise and shine, and nations shall turn to her light and kings to the brightness of her rising. Then the mountain of the house of the Lord will rise above all the mountains, and all the nations will flow to it. What an exalted position his church will have! God wants every precious stone tested, tried, safe, secure and able to handle the glory as well as the pressure.

So the church will be full of genuinely meek people who know that left to themselves they are weak and helpless. Jesus, our meek and lowly King, is calling an army of believers who have no confidence in the flesh.

When we go through pressure we often feel 'storm-tossed, afflicted and not comforted' and some even question their salvation. We can miss God's purpose if we are not careful. There are three wrong ways in which to respond. Firstly, it says in Hebrews 12:5, 'My son, *do not regard lightly* the discipline of the Lord.' Don't shrug it off and fail to respond to God's dealings with you. Secondly, '[*Don't*] *faint* when you are reproved by him,' as some children do when you correct them. They retort, 'You are always against me!' and collapse in self-pity. Thirdly, the writer to the Hebrews warns us to *make sure that no root of bitterness grows up*, spoiling many (see Heb 12:15).

God is training us. Pressure is of benefit to those who are trained by it!

## A fruitful vine by a spring

How did Joseph survive? What made him victorious through the whole experience? Genesis 49:22 describes Joseph as a fruitful vine by a spring, whose branches went over the wall. What a beautiful testimony! And so reminiscent of Jeremiah 17:7–8,

> Blessed is the man...whose trust is the Lord. For he will be like a tree planted by the water, that extends its roots by a stream and will not fear when the heat comes; but its leaves will be green, and it will not be anxious in a year of drought nor cease to yield fruit.

The tree that sends its roots down into the stream does not fear when the heat comes. Though Joseph was in furnace conditions, his roots were in the stream. He was still trusting God. Not only did he continue to bear fruit, but his bough climbed up over the wall. He not only kept himself, he blessed those around him, whether it was Potiphar's household or his fellow prisoners. In spite of his own needs, he noticed when the baker and the butler were distressed and asked, 'Why is your countenance down? Why do you look sad?' He still had something to give away. He had grace for himself and for others.

## Unwavering faith

In addition to this, Joseph retained his confidence in God and childlike faith in the promise of his original visions. How do I know that he kept believing? Because of his response to the baker and the butler when they told Joseph about their dreams. How easily he could have replied, 'I used to have dreams! If I were you, I would forget it! I had dreams, but I've grown up now'—but he didn't! Immediately he replied, 'Tell my your dreams; I will tell you the interpretation!' No cynicism, no disillusionment. Joseph was still believing. Since he had had his dreams everything had gone wrong, but he never foreclosed on God. He still believed! If he was willing to interpret for others he must still have been confident in his own dream. He did not hesitate. He spoke out of confident faith, not out of bitter frustration and disillusionment.

The psalmist said, 'I believed, therefore have I spoken' (Ps 116:10, AV). Perhaps you have been going through a test and the promise you were given seems so far in the past. Everything has gone so wrong. Have you jettisoned the word that gripped and thrilled you or are you, like Joseph, still as confident in the word God gave you as when you first heard it? God wants us to speak because we believe. The heat is not to destroy our faith but to refine it.

May God deliver us from throwing away our confidence. We must be followers of those who through faith and patience inherited the promises, and we must let God's furnace refine and prepare us for the ministry that he has for us in the future. Psalm 105 tells us that the word of the Lord tested Joseph until the word came to pass. It was certain that the promise of God would 'come to pass'. Joseph had endured the test and was about to step onto centre stage. He was about to come from obscurity into the fulfilment of God's promises. Tested, tried and found faithful.

# 6

## *From Prison to Palace*

Eventually the time came for Joseph's release and the fulfilment of his early vision. At last he was liberated from those confining, restricting walls, to emerge centre stage in the world's limelight. But what actually caused his release?

First of all *God promised* that it would happen. The story started with a definite promise from God, who revealed his purpose by giving the young Joseph two visions. (God has also declared that he will glorify his Son through his church, so that will happen too!)

Secondly, it was because of *Joseph's persevering faith-fulness*. He could have disqualified himself time and again, but he remained steadfast. In absolute integrity he passed from test to test and was changed from one degree of glory to another. God wants us to mature like that. As you are poured from one vessel to another, don't complain but believe that God makes all things work together for good!

Thirdly, he emerged because of *his life in the Spirit*. He was still living in his spiritual anointing, using the gifts God had given him. He still interpreted dreams. He did not waste his marvellous gift from God, so God unbolted doors for him. The butler suddenly remembered a man whom he met in prison, who lived in a different dimension—not shut into this world's ignorance and barrenness. The supernatural gifts will also provide the breakthrough for the church in these end times. Already we are seeing people previously closed to the gospel opening their hearts as a result of such spiritual gifts as words of knowledge and healings. Sinners seem more impressed by the supernatural than they are with things being done pleasantly, decently, or with great aesthetic beauty and skill. No one can deny that the church looks stunningly impressive at such occasions as royal weddings, yet the sobering truth is that few are beating on the doors of the church afterwards saying, 'It was so impressive that you must show us how we can know God like that!'

Beautifully organized occasions are not the answer to life's needs. No, we need the anointing of God to open up the way. Pharaoh recognized it, and said that Joseph was a man in whom there was a divine Spirit. That was Joseph's hallmark and it must become the mark of the church— men in whom there is the divine Spirit! Joseph was a mature young man, thirty years of age now, and no longer that abrasive seventeen year old. God is likewise going to mature his church to the fullness of the stature of Christ. Corporately the church must step upon the stage as a people in whom dwells the divine Spirit.

## Not me, but God

Joseph came out of his furnace in intimate communion with God. The Egyptians challenged him: 'We understand that you can interpret dreams,' and at once he replied, 'It is not in me, but God will.' Immediately they encountered God, not merely a man. God forbid that we should go into the furnace if we do not come out knowing God better. Paul said that our pressures are to teach us not to trust in ourselves but in God who raises the dead (2 Cor 1:9). We lose our *self*-confidence as the furnace shows us what rubbish we are and we discover what God knew about us from the beginning. Joseph emerged with great confidence in his God.

Still a young man, he could have thought, as many pagans of his day did, that there was a god of the mountains and a god of the valleys, a god of Egypt and a god of Canaan. Facing the challenge of Egypt, he could have regarded his 'family religion' as totally inadequate in different circumstances. Many young people become vulnerable when wondering if their parents' faith will be adequate to face the challenges of a modern university, but Joseph did not surface with such second-hand faith. He boldly declared, 'My God will intervene. He rules over everything and has determined these events.' So mighty Pharaoh met with Almighty God!

Joseph had a clear understanding that his father's God and his God was King of the nations. Those of you who go to schools where people don't believe in your father's God, do you feel defensive when your teachers are sceptical and your friends even more so? You can become apologetic about your beliefs. Joseph did not, however. He believed that his God was as much Master of mighty Egypt as he was of lowly Canaan. Wherever Joseph was, be it Potiphar's house or prison, or now before mighty Pharaoh, he was confident in God. Our generation waits to see people who know God in the same way; who do not confront them only with their personal opinions, but speak boldly about their Christian faith in God.

Today we often hear people complaining that they don't know what is happening to the nation. Too often we quickly agree that the nation is in a terrible condition. By God's grace and by his Spirit being upon us, we need to explain that the nation has turned its back on God and that is why we have missed the way. We must confront our atheistic nation with the God in whom we believe.

**Famine conditions**

Joseph immediatly brought the presence of God into the centre of Pharaoh's predicament. He had dreamed of seven prosperous years followed by seven years of famine. Psalm 105:16 makes an extraordinary statement: '[God] called for a famine upon the land.' Again, we see God's awe-inspiring providence. The story started when God caused some Ishmaelites to be moving south to Egypt on the very day that the brothers turned against Joseph. God called for those Ishmaelites and now God called for the famine. Just as we might call a dog, God can summon a famine. He rules over all!

Today we are living in days of terrible famine. People do not know which way to turn. There are worldwide economic pressures which neither politicians nor economists can solve. Not very long ago we were told that we had 'never had it so good', but now we have millions out of work, and it would appear that things are going to get worse.

A terrible moral famine is also stalking through our land. The nation is morally bankrupt. There is a famine in the arts. Much of our music, theatre and painting seems to reflect emptiness and pessimism. A very close friend of mine studied at Brighton College of Art. Having completed his degree course, he gave me the dubious pleasure of looking at the work of his fellow students as they completed their three-year degree course. As I walked around the Art College, I came to the conclusion that there is indeed a famine in the land! To think that what I saw was the product of years of training! The very atmosphere of the College and encounters with the students only strengthened my verdict. The dreary depressing work filling the rooms and hanging on the walls was how the young minds had expressed their 'famine' on paper and canvas.

There is a famine of fresh ideas, a famine of skill, a

famine of steadfastness, a famine of integrity and, the greatest famine of all, a famine of the teaching of God's word. The worst thing that can ever happen to a nation is for God not to speak any more. In Romans 1 we see a terrible phrase occurring three times: 'God gave them up.' When people have refused, rejected and turned their backs, sometimes God gives them up.

Hell is a place where God will never speak again!

There is a dearth of the word of God being faithfully and powerfully proclaimed in our land and it is leading to moral decadence right across the nation. In Joseph's day God called for a famine and what used to be healthy and strong was destroyed. The nation's resources were plundered. But wonderfully, on this occasion, the famine was to provide the awful backcloth to the painting of mercy and grace which God was about to paint upon it. He created the famine to highlight the resources which Joseph would provide. We must pray that as darkness covers the earth and gross darkness the people, God will cause the light of the church to arise in amazing contrast. If we will clearly focus on God, and his wonderful promises of grace and mercy, we need not panic at the famine but believe in the almighty God who overrules all history. It was in this context that Joseph was prepared. His God-given wisdom would revolutionize the situation.

# 7

## *Food for All*

Joseph could simply have been delivered from prison and that could have been the end of the story, but instead his deliverance from prison prepared the way for the deliverance of a nation from famine! Joseph stood in the centre of Pharaoh's court and prophesied that prosperity would be followed by famine. In a few years the country would be hit by disaster and he held the key—not only to Egypt's survival but to that of the surrounding nations as well!

He arrived with all the answers to the needs of his generation, and God plans the same for his church today. He has invested in the church all that is required. The principles of the kingdom of God provide the answers to all nations' needs. He is teaching us wonderful principles that the man in the street has never heard, never grasped, never seen and never thought possible. He has taught us about integrity, family life, the essential covenant of love between husband and wife. He has taught us that security and peace are the results of a marriage where a wife honours and recognizes her husband's headship and where the husband unselfishly loves and honours his wife. This generation has been duped by cries of 'Liberation for women!' only to find itself more entangled and confused than before.

Another life-changing principle which God is teaching us is that children who are undisciplined are unloved. If we love our children we will patiently teach them how to behave, how to respect others. We will teach them principles and morality based on God's word. We will not let them run wild and unrestrained so that they become obnoxious to society, selfish and lawless, unable to make relationships or have any self-respect, security or sense of dignity.

When one of our sons had a party to celebrate his sixth birthday, he invited along half a dozen little boys and we organized some games. After a fairly energetic afternoon, parents came to fetch their children. We told one mother that we had been playing games with the boys and she was plainly surprised. 'But they don't like that sort of thing these days. When we have them for a party we say, "Do what you like," and then just hold on for a couple of hours until its all over!' Actually, however, these boys did enjoy organized games. This surprised the lady, first, because we took the time and trouble to organize the games, and secondly, because they actually enjoyed it!

God has been showing us principles that the modern world has abandoned. He has told us about honesty at work, integrity in our employment, a proper work ethic with workmen doing a good day's work and honouring their masters, and masters being honest instead of manipulating the labour in order to get the best out of them and destroying them in the process. The Bible teaches responsibility on every side. These are the wonderful laws of the kingdom—the wisdom of God for how to live on his planet.

We have also been learning how to be a covenant-keeping community in an age when covenant is easily cast aside. We are finding joy through living righteously in a world that is as miserable as sin. We ought to use that phrase frequently! Let's talk about being 'as miserable as sin' so that people will hear and understand that *sin is essentially miserable* and that God has caused us to find joy through righteousness! Tragically, unbelievers have often regarded Christians as killjoys. It is time they discovered that we are 'have-joys'.

When Joseph was confronted by the prospect of famine he stored up everything the people would need to see them through the national emergency. God is similarly storing up all the necessary resources in his church. He has given us kingdom principles. He has shared with us his own wisdom.

## Open the storehouses!

Joseph fulfilled his calling by opening up his storehouses to minister to the nation's need. As the famine spread over all the face of the earth, Joseph threw open Egypt's vast resources (Gen 41:56). The nation was in dire need and Joseph had all the answers. The people poured in to buy grain from Joseph. Joseph was truly a prophetic figure. We started our story by noting that in the last days 'your old men will dream dreams, your young men will see visions' (Joel 2:28). But we should also notice that:

> In the last days,
> The mountain of the house of the Lord
> Will be established as the chief of the mountains,
> And will be raised above the hills;
> And all the nations will stream to it.
> And many peoples will come and say,
> 'Come, let us go up to the mountain of the Lord,
> To the house of the God of Jacob;
> That He may teach us concerning His ways,
> And that we may walk in His paths.'
> For the law will go forth from Zion,
> And the word of the Lord from Jerusalem.
> And He will judge between the nations,
> And will render decisions for many peoples.
> (Is 2:2)

There it is! In the last days God will cause the mountain of the house of the Lord, that great Zion about which we so often sing, to be raised above the other mountains. The other 'mountains' will not be able to come up with the answers—political, economic or social. Whatever their philosophy they will not be able to provide the answer. But the mountain of the house of the Lord will appear above the other mountains and all the nations will say, 'There is grain there. Those Christians have found how to live. Let us go!' God has promised that this will happen. The unsaved will say, 'Let us go up to the mountain of the Lord...that He may teach us about His ways' (Mic 4:2). People in our streets whose marriages are in desperate straits; who don't know how to look after their children; who are in financial trouble; who are confronted by so many different problems, will begin to seek us out. Ordinary people like you and me who have been through the furnace, through the testing, will be seen as a corporate testimony in our towns. And people will come and ask us how it is we are so happy and fulfilled and how is it that our families are so secure.

Isaiah 60:1–5 underlines the same amazing promise:

> Arise, shine; for your light has come,
> And the glory of the Lord has risen upon you.
> For behold, darkness will cover the earth,
> And deep darkness the peoples;

[This is another way of saying that there is going to be a great moral famine.]

> But the Lord will arise upon you,
> And His glory will appear upon you.
> And nations will come to your light,
> And kings to the brightness of your rising.
> Lift up your eyes round about, and see;
> They all gather together, they come to you.
> Your sons will come from afar,

And your daughters will be carried in the arms.
Then you will see and be radiant,
And your heart will thrill and rejoice.

In the last days, God will bring forth a marvellous,
mature, 'Joseph company', with answers for the famine.
People will stream in. Even Joseph's own brothers began
to hear. He was no longer perceived to be the arrogant,
abrasive teenager, flaunting his spiritual visions. He now
appeared with maturity and wisdom, having grain in the
midst of famine.

## Brotherly love triumphs!

How did Joseph fulfil his calling? He graciously received
his brothers. Indeed, the way in which he received them is
one of the most beautiful parts of the whole story. He did
not turn on them, nor did he say, 'You threw me out, but
now I have the upper hand!' No, Joseph was genuinely
thrilled that his brothers wanted to come. There was no
resentment, no bitterness, no keeping them at arm's
length. He loved them. At first, he did not reveal his
identity, but when he saw them his heart went out to
them. He was so moved that he hurriedly left the room to
weep in private. Eventually, the moment came for dis-
closure—'I am Joseph, your brother.' Amazed and fearful, they backed away, fearing his revenge, but he called
them to come closer and reassured them, 'You meant evil
against me, but God meant it for good in order to...
preserve many people alive' (Gen 50:20). Then he threw
his arms around them and kissed them and they wept and
talked together.

Some of you were asked to leave churches because you
saw visions, prophesied and spoke with tongues. Will you
be as open as Joseph? God's purpose was for all his sons.
His plans were for the whole nation of Israel. It was in fact
from *Judah* rather than Joseph that God's ultimate pur-

pose would emerge. Do not think that because you had a vision you are special. No! God sent a man ahead that he might save them all. His heart was for them all, and God's heart is for all his beloved children whether they receive your visions and dreams or not, whether they accept your charismatic testimony or not. God's heart is for everyone whom he has purchased with the blood of his Son, for he loves them all and sees them all partaking in his glorious purpose.

In recent years, a growing number have stepped out of the clutter of irrelevant tradition and, unrestricted by lifeless formality, they have been freed to rediscover some of the basic essentials required for building a church that will reach their generation. Already the world is beginning to say, 'These churches really speak my language. They are not pushing religion at me—they have something I want. They seem to love each other. They are a community, sharing their possessions and giving to one another. Their faith does not seem to be confined to special buildings on special days.' Growing numbers are beginning to be saved and are sharing this kind of a testimony.

Joseph was able to feed the people in a time of famine, but that was not all. Psalm 105:21 says quite plainly that Pharaoh made him lord of his house and ruler over all his possessions, with authority to imprison Pharaoh's princes at will. Joseph exercised real authority in Pharaoh's world. God is not simply raising up his church to feed the nations; he is bringing in a kingdom where the government of Jesus is clearly seen—a kingdom where Jesus is Lord. The people of God are to be formed into an army which wages spiritual warfare and learns 'to bind their kings with chains, and their nobles with fetters of iron; to execute on them the judgment written; this is an honor for all His godly ones' (Ps 149:8–9). The church must demonstrate the rule and government of Christ.

Even now we are seated with Christ in heavenly places

on his throne, sharing his authority. God told his Son long ago, 'Sit at My right hand, until I make Thine enemies a footstool for Thy feet' (Ps 110:1). (The Old Testament verse most quoted in the New Testament.) Jesus will be seen as a mighty King in and through his people, with him as our Head in heaven and with us his people on earth. People will come from every nation to hear the ways of God. Jesus is the Saviour of *all* men, especially those who believe (1 Tim 4:10). *All* men, not only believers, will benefit from the vast reservoirs of God's grace as Egypt benefited from Joseph's life-saving work.

We are reminded in 1 Corinthians 15:24–28 that one day Jesus will return, 'Then comes the end, when He delivers up the kingdom to the God and Father, when He has abolished all rule and all authority and power. For He must reign until He has put all His enemies under His feet.'

What a glorious consummation of the ages when there is a worldwide expression of the government of Jesus and then he hands over the rule to his Father, having subjected all authority to himself. By God's grace let us be partners with him in his great plan of redemption and bring everlasting glory to the Lamb!

# GIDEON

'... whose weakness was
turned to strength; and who
became powerful in battle and
routed foreign armies'
(Heb 11:34, NIV).

# 8

## *Sitting in Darkness*

The sky was black. The passengers dozed uncomfortably as the plane flew on through the night. I lifted the blind and stared out at the dense darkness. Gradually, I became aware that a change was taking place. It was as if someone had taken a razor blade and made a gigantic cut on the Eastern horizon. An orange line appeared and, as the perfectly straight line widened, light poured through in increasing intensity of golden brilliance. Dawn was breaking across the sky, overcoming the night.

'The people who walk in darkness will see a great light.' So begins one of the best-known prophecies in Isaiah. As it continues a picture unfolds of a time when God's nation shall be multiplied, the yoke of slavery broken, and a new government will emerge.

It will be an ever-increasing government, resting comfortably on the shoulders of a child born to us, whose name will be called Wonderful Counsellor, Mighty God, Everlasting Father, Prince of Peace—and there will be no end to the increase of his government (Is 9:2–7). Wonderful promises herald the coming of the King and his kingdom.

We live in days of the kingdom's advance. Jesus said this gospel of the kingdom must be preached to all nations before the end comes. Through the ages men and women have carried the baton in their generation. Now our time has come. Ultimately, the light of the kingdom will be seen by all the nations who sit in darkness. A time of significant breakthrough must come!

But how will it come? What can we expect? Isaiah 9:4 gives us an unexpected clue when it tells us it will be 'as at the battle of Midian'. So if we want to find out how light overcomes darkness, and what happens when the light of God explodes into a world that has grown accustomed to shadows, confusion and blindness, we need to look at this battle of Midian. There we shall discover important lessons that are particularly relevant today as we look for God's power to break out through the spiritual darkness of our own generation.

At that time the Israelites were also living in 'darkness' (see Judges 6). They were in hiding, overwhelmed by their enemies and lacking any sense of the blessing of God resting upon them. However, by the end of chapter 7 the defeated nation had been transformed into a victorious people. Clearly, these chapters contain crucially important principles that we cannot afford to overlook.

The story begins with a description of one of the most devastating scenes of Israel in the Old Testament. They lived in constant fear of the raiding Midianite armies. Repeated savage attacks had eventually forced them into hiding, and they began living in mountain caves. Every time they planted seeds in the valley, their enemies would invade and destroy the entire crop. The once-conquering nation of Israel therefore had gradually fallen into a period of terrible decline. It seemed as though the enemies of Israel were invincible. Nothing could be done about them. Before long the Israelites had to adapt to simply existing under great pressure and eventually they resorted to hiding.

Now the tragedy in Gideon's day was that this people, these sons of Israel, were God's people. They were a people of great destiny and of a magnificent past. The previous generations under Moses and Joshua had known outstanding victories and triumphs. They had experienced many outbreakings of the supernatural power of God. They had seen the Red Sea separate; they had seen the walls of Jericho crumble. That was their immediate history. They also had a glorious future. The next generation would see the anointing of Samuel, leading on to the mighty kingdoms of David and Solomon.

But during the period spanned by the book of Judges, there was a desperate spiritual trough. A tragic time between a miraculous past and a glorious future. It was tragic because it was also a charismatic era when God showed himself willing to pour out his Spirit on individuals. What a tragedy to live in such a time, among a people of such calling, who were yet without purpose or hope. God's mighty power was available to them, yet they lived without any obvious sense of his blessing.

How relevant this story is to the church in our nation today. We are seen as an irrelevant body lacking both strength and purpose; a tiny percentage of the population, a remnant from a previous age. A national newspaper recently recorded its appraisal of the modern minister as follows: 'He is a general dogsbody looking after a group of well-meaning but generally harmless people.'

This is hardly how the New Testament describes the church but, nonetheless, most people would settle for it in describing today's church.

In today's church people are looking at the serious needs of our land, but arriving at so many different answers. As in Gideon's day, truth formerly believed and obeyed has been abandoned and men are doing what is right in their own eyes. A minister told me recently that he had attended a local conference for his particular denomination where it was suggested that the reason people do not come into churches any more is because we are so full of ourselves. We arrogantly invite people to come and hear us. Surely we should change our style and say that all men are seeking God? We should invite non-Christians to discussions instead of services and share ideas in our common search for God. To his horror, the suggestion was received with much enthusiasm! They thought this was a great idea!

Most people regard today's church as hopelessly ana-chronistic and offering no relevant answers. Meanwhile, our enemies are gaining ground—or at least it would appear so. In my home town of Brighton there have been major spiritualist conferences, and conventions for all manner of groups involved in the occult. We see our enemies gaining ground while the church remains insig-nificant, apparently with no answer, with no word for the situation, just hiding in caves.

In this country we can also look back to times when God has moved powerfully. Many Christians also believe that he will do so once again, for we are convinced that it is God's purpose to bring his church to the fullness of the stature of Christ. We are confident that God is going to prepare his bride until she is without spot or wrinkle, ready for Jesus. We have been privileged with a wonderful history and a glorious future awaits us. Are we content merely to live through a spiritual trough and fail to move God in our generation?

This is the setting for the story of Gideon and God has made special mention of it in Isaiah 9. The marvellous increase of government shall be 'as the battle of Midian'.

### How it all began

It all started during a time of spiritual decline, but first we must see just why and how the nation arrived at such a low state. A simple explanation would be that the Midianites were too strong. Overwhelmed, the Israelites had retreated to the caves. That is the *simple* answer.

A more sophisticated interpretation put forward in

some commentaries is that they had been defeated by a new secret weapon that they had never encountered before—a new problem that they had never faced! A secret weapon of great speed and with the ability to strike suddenly—the camel! The Midianite army, with the aid of camels, presented problems that Israel had never before encountered in warfare. It was because of the camel, some would have us believe, that Israel fell into decline.

Actually, if we look closely, we find that neither the Midianite nation nor their 'secret weapon' provides us with the real answer. It would be lunacy to assume that the God who dealt with the Red Sea and mighty Jericho found his match in a camel! No! The fact that they were overrun was a demonstration that their problem was not with the Midianites at all, but with God himself.

### The real problem

Chapter 6 begins: 'Then the sons of Israel did what was evil in the sight of the Lord; and *the Lord* gave them into the hands of Midian seven years.'

It was not that their enemies were too great but rather that God was not with them. More than that, it says in Judges 2:15, 'Wherever they went, the hand of the Lord was against them for evil.' God was, therefore, actively against his own people. It further says, 'The Lord strengthened Eglon the king of Moab against Israel' (3:12). In reading the Old Testament we find that God often strengthened Israel's pagan enemies when Israel turned away from him—a fact that bewildered Habakkuk and a truth that Jeremiah had to live with throughout his entire ministry.

Therefore, the Israelites were defeated and living in caves—not because God's strength was insufficient to help them—rather because God was so mighty! Ruling in heaven and on earth he was strengthening their enemies!

**What about today?**

How do these circumstances speak to our situation today?
Some would argue that the church is not prospering today
because of new problems which we have never had to face
before. We have to contend with the vast pressure of a
secular society, humanist teaching in our schools and the
continual brainwashing by television and the media. Some
would list other modern-day 'camels' that prevent the
church from prospering, such as communism, spiritualism
or 'scientific' atheism. Some feel that the church simply
cannot cope with the problems of the late twentieth
century. The implication is that somehow God cannot
keep up with modern trends!

Scripture, however, teaches us something very different, namely that God will even strengthen enemies against
his people when they are not honouring him. We must not
be tempted to think this was a situation confined to the
Old Testament. God has never said that he will be with his
people in any circumstance and at all costs. Our God is a
holy God. He gives his Holy Spirit *to those who obey him*.
He answers the prayers of *the righteous* and he will cause
the devil to flee *if we humble ourselves* before him. We
know that God gives grace to the humble, but *he opposes
the proud*! This truth is written in a letter to *his own
people*. God will *oppose* the proud. He will also oppose
lying and cheating—even in his New Testament church.
He removed Ananias and Sapphira for that very reason.
Paul wrote to the church at Corinth: 'Some of you are sick
and some have even died,' when they abused the Lord's
Supper. God judged them. The church in sin does not
merely miss out on blessing, but actually experiences the
opposition of Almighty God.

So often we assume that it is the devil who closes down
churches. When we hear of church buildings being converted into warehouses or bought by other religions we
regard it as the devil's work. But the New Testament says

that Jesus stands in the middle of the candlesticks and says, 'I will remove this one or close that one.' God has never left his throne! He is to be feared. He will have his people as they are meant to be, otherwise he will oppose them. He will not bless willy-nilly!

As the government of Jesus increases, God will have deep dealings with his people. Jesus is not merely gentle and mild, he is also the God of wrath and judgement. Look, for example, at the early chapters of the book of Revelation. Old Testament or New, he remains the same true God. If you read through the second chapter of Revelation in which Jesus is speaking to his churches, you see such words of judgement as: 'I have this against you...Remember therefore from where you have fallen, and repent...or else I am coming to you, and will remove your lampstand out of its place' (vv. 4–5). Jesus goes on to threaten 'war', 'sickness' and 'tribulation' against the various churches should they refuse to repent.

This is our mighty God. We cannot just carry on as we want and hope God will bless us. Neither can we plead special excuses for the difficult days in which we live. How many people have you met who say, 'Of course our town is a very difficult one—a real centre for witchcraft'? But no town is too difficult for our God. He stands above it all. The Lord Jesus said, 'All authority has been given to Me in heaven and on earth' (Mt 28:18). But he also said, 'I have this against you....'

That was the situation in Gideon's day. Their defeat was not due to the power of the enemy at all! God had some things against them. God also has some things against his church today which he is putting right. We need to know what they are and to respond diligently. There are two possibilities open to us when God isn't blessing us. We can either settle for the status quo, or we can cry to God.

**Another generation**

In Gideon's day there were those who chose simply to get
used to the situation. They really had not known, first
hand at least, that it could be any different. A tragic
phrase in Judges 2 shows us that those of the great generation who had seen Jericho fall were all dead. 'There arose
another generation after them who did not know the
Lord, nor yet the work which He had done for Israel'
(Judg 2:10). They themselves had never seen his power
manifest.

On the whole, we too have grown up in a generation
that has not seen the mighty acts of God as our forefathers
did. We have not seen the revivals during which thousands
flocked into the churches to get right with God. Unlike
our fathers, we have not known whole towns changed,
with demonstrations of power and incredible mani-
festations of the glory of God. Our generation, in the
main, knows nothing of these things. We may closely
identify with the Israel of Gideon's day.

Finding that God was not with them, many of his people
simply dug in—living in holes on the mountains. It was the
more pitiful since mountains are supposed to typify significant places for strategic possession. When under Joshua
they began to move into the promised land, the mountains
stood for the heights of authority and power. Caleb, for
his reward, sought a mountain. In warfare, to be on top of
the mountain was to be in the place of great authority.
The mountains also feature in psalms of praise: get up into
a high mountain and say, 'Behold your God.' The mountains were to be possessed, but this generation dug in and
'made for themselves the dens which were in the mountains' (Judg 6:2).

In a similar way, you can either possess a great truth of
God or you can dig in and hide behind it. There were such
people in Jesus' day. They said, 'We are children of
Abraham.' Abraham to them was a mountain-figure of

faith, but the faith he lived by, they never knew. When Jesus came to them, he ushered in a new day of the Spirit, a new demonstration of the power of God. But they said, 'No, we are sons of Abraham, we received the law from Moses.' They might have said, 'No, our doctrine is sound.'

Likewise, we often take great truths from the Bible and, instead of living in the good of them, we dig in defensively and hide behind them. The result is that instead of saying, 'God is faithful, let us therefore bring in the kingdom,' we say, 'God is faithful. I will defend that truth to the end.'

When I was at Bible College, we were taught that the great objective was to be 'sound'. We were sound and we were going to show the modern liberal theologians where they were not sound! We were also taught to beware of any undue emphasis of doctrine. We were safe and careful and the great key word was 'balance'. Balance was the thing we sought to defend. If anybody got too excited, that was moving into emotionalism. As a friend of mine wrote mockingly in a College magazine: 'As we worship this great God of soundness and balance, with both feet firmly on the ground, let us go forward.'

So we find that the 'sound' men of Jesus' day were always on the defensive. They took offence at the disciples' neglect of ceremonial washings. Time after time, they spoke out against Jesus as they sought to protect the truth as they understood it; the rules behind which they hid.

By contrast, in Caleb's day, they laid hold of the truth. They argued, 'If God is faithful, as the word says, let us go and take the land.' Their doctrine was a source of confidence—more a springboard than a dug-out! But Gideon's generation, not having seen God's power for themselves, fell into the temptation just to dig in and hide in the mountain caves. There is no time for 'digging in' defensively. It's time to get onto the offensive and take God at his word.

First of all, however, we must put our own house in order. Our individual lives must come under scrutiny and so must the way we run the church of the living God. I believe God wants his church back! He wants it to be run in his own way.

May God deliver us from defending cold orthodoxy. Rather let us be orthodox like Caleb, by obeying God and proving him as we believe his infallible word and put it into action.

# 9

## *The Prophet Explains*

If to 'dig in' is one option when God is not blessing the church, the other quite simply is to cry to God. But what should we cry? There are many today who are beginning to cry to the Lord—a great body of prayer warriors is beginning to stir up across the country—but what do we pray?

Do we pray, 'God smash the Midianites'? Jesus' contemporaries wanted to pray, 'O God, break the Roman yoke.' So also we might be tempted to pray, 'O Lord, break through against the spiritualists, communists,' or whatever. But this is not the prayer that God is waiting to hear, for it is not where the problem lies. What they ought to have prayed for, and what we must seek God for, is revealed by the answer God gave. When they began to cry out to God, he supplied three answers: a prophetic explanation, an anointed leadership and a committed army. That was God's response then and that is what he wants to do in our day.

Praying against spiritualists and occult conferences is only attacking pimples on the surface. Our problem is not simply with the enemy, our problem is with God who wants to speak to us through a prophetic voice. That is what he did in David's day. He sent the prophet Samuel, who in turn anointed fresh leadership before a committed army was gathered under David. The formula was repeated in Jesus' day. First came John the Baptist, then our anointed Saviour, and ultimately came the committed army.

The prophetic message brought to Gideon's generation reminded them firstly that they were a covenant people. He said, 'I brought you out of Egypt. I delivered you against powerful forces. The Egyptians were far too powerful for you so I delivered you and brought you into the land but you have not obeyed me. You did not drive out your enemies.'

Throughout the book of Judges, God repeatedly challenged them. Although God had performed such wonders for his people, they had not obeyed him. They were supposed to drive out the enemy forces, with all their evil practices, but Israel learned to live with them. Then after a while we find them not only coexisting with the Canaanites, but actually worshipping their gods. Spiritual adultery! They were meant to come into the land, purge the land of evil and establish the kingdom of God. Instead, they settled, got used to the evil going on around them and eventually accepted those standards. Worst of all, they grieved the Lord by bowing down to the Amorite idols (6:10), the false gods of that age.

God would raise the same issues with his church today. Our present weakness and lack of power is not so much to do with the strength of our enemies as our spiritual adultery. Our God remains the same holy God and he would say, 'Deliver yourselves from the gods all around you. Step right out and be a people for me and you will see my power and glory in your own day.'

## Modern idols

What are the false gods we worship today? There are many, but I would like to mention two or three specifically.

Money dominates today's society. So many spend their lives and energies striving for more and more. During the

Sermon on the Mount, Jesus said quite simply that you cannot serve God and money. If you serve money, you will eventually be ensnared in the cares of this world and they will preoccupy you and bring you into bondage.

Jesus said, 'Where your treasure is, there will your heart be also' (Mt 6:21). How many of us who say 'Money has no power over me,' would give up the offer of promotion and prospects in another region in order to remain where God was using us? If the job offered was in a town where there was no dynamic, living, Spirit-filled fellowship, would we go? It is easy to say, 'There's bound to be a church there,' but we all know that in these days there are churches and churches. It is easy to say, 'We'll see what we can find when we get there,' but that is actually putting the kingdom of God second. Jesus told us to seek first the kingdom of God and his righteousness (Mt 6:33). Do we make our decisions according to his standards or according to the standards all around us?

We have seen those who have put career first and as a result have lost the way. Their spiritual life has declined and their children have grown up robbed of a living church.

Our heart attitude regarding money is also tested by our reaction to giving. Many would say, 'What with inflation and my mortgage and other financial commitments, I can't really afford to give. I give what I can, but tithing is ridiculous.' But Jesus said, 'Give, and it will be given to you; good measure, pressed down, shaken together, running over' (Lk 6:38). Jesus said, 'Do not fear—give!' It's a different way of life. It defies the gods of this world. The gods of this world warn you to hold on or you will be in a terrible state when you get to the end of the month. Jesus, however, is a different kind of king. He says, 'Give and it will be given to you.' He says that he who obeys these words will have solid rock foundations to his life and not treacherous sands. God has written principles that defy the world. Proverbs 11:24 says, 'There is one who scatters, yet increases all the more. And there is one who

withholds what is justly due, but it results only in want.'
Those who would say, 'I can't give at the moment, I can't
afford it,' are not responding to the voice of God, but to
the gods of this world.

## Kingdom treasure

The kingdom of God is like a man who found treasure in a
field and said, 'I'll sell everything else I have in order to
possess that field. Everything else must go, I must have
the treasure. I must have the kingdom of God. I want to
be in the kingdom where God moves with power. I want
to see the demonstration of the glory of Jesus. I want my
dear Saviour who bled and died and was exalted and
glorified. I want to be in his kingdom. I will not throw it
away for a mess of pottage. I am not going to throw it
away by making secular considerations. I have found
something that is worth everything. That's the pearl of
great price and I will let everything go to obtain it; everything, in order to be in the centre of his will.'

How is it with you? That's the standard that Jesus
talked about. He said that's how it is when people follow
him. He gave everything to possess us and he wants us to
show the same response. He wants a bride caught up in
the magnitude of his love, not a people ensnared in the
cares of this world.

One of the things God used to provoke me into full-
time ministry was a meeting with a young Jehovah's
Witness. He was financing himself by window cleaning
each morning so that he could go out door-knocking with
his message in the afternoons. I thought, 'Here am I,
giving all my time to work and travelling to work, but this
fellow has given everything to serve in a miserable cult.'

God is looking for a whole army that will arise with this
clear priority—the pearl which is above price. Our goal is
not how much we can get away with, or how much we can
hold on to. It's not, 'Shall I tithe before or after tax?' Nor is

it seeking first your career, your home or your prospects. It is a totally different attitude. Jesus said that if we cannot be clear about this, we will never make progress with him, for we cannot serve both God and money.

## Preoccupation with sex

The second powerful god around us today was also worshipped in Gideon's generation. The goddess Ashtoreth, among other evil practices, was a goddess of sexual perversion. Our generation also is obsessed by sex, and numberless lives are held in its grip.

I have heard some of you younger people say, 'But it's so hard today. At school everyone talks about it. I get laughed at. Only two or three of us in my class are still virgins. I do mean to marry my boyfriend one day and I'm sure that God understands. I suppose we have let the standards drop a bit.'

God's standards have never changed and yet so many in his church have given in to the pressure to follow the world. So many have let their purity go because of an ugly, ensnaring god that prevails in our land today. But God has given us everything we need for life and godliness (2 Pt 1:3). We must not, and need not, serve other gods. God wants us to be free. He wants us to be holy. He wants our standards to be bright and clear.

Of course, it is not only the young who are pressured by this god. People in their middle years will often have to face new areas of temptation and pressure. People with unconverted husbands or wives find warmth of friendship with other Christians in the church. Suddenly and unexpectedly, they find themselves lured and under pressure. But God will not own a people who bow down to this god.

In the book of Revelation, Jesus spoke against a church that allowed adultery. His burning gaze penetrated the situation. With a sword proceeding from his mouth, he will deal with his church regarding the worship of other gods. He sees it as spiritual adultery. It is obeying the power of the world, following its gods, giving in to its ways.

Jesus is seeking faithfulness among his people, his bride. We must live in purity before him. God wants us to be free from this ugly god of sexual sin that stalks our land. He wants his people to be holy and free. It is not enough for us to say, 'Everyone else is doing it.' We have got to be free. Young people especially, you must stand up in these days and through God's power be free from these pressures.

## Foolish wisdom

The third god that confronts us today is 'wordly wisdom', a god that has always attempted to creep into the church. Paul spelt out the enmity between the gospel and worldly wisdom, teaching that the gospel of the cross is folly to the world—it is foolishness! The wordly-wise man of today thinks he has outgrown a gospel of a cross and shed blood. He would much rather speak philosophically. He is too intellectual for such primitive nonsense!

A god of worldly wisdom is, in some ways, a subtle one. Yet how willingly many Christians yield to its pressure. Because some of the things God speaks of in his word are not easily understood, we begin to cut our cloth. Rather than be outspoken with the foolishness of our message, we make things acceptable for the modern man.

Many are doing this today, even with the current outpouring of the Holy Spirit. They speak in tongues and rejoice in their new experiences, but they restrict them to a back room on Wednesday night. Meanwhile, the Sunday meeting is reserved for modern man. A nice, ordered service calculated to offend no one. That's where worldly wisdom comes in—don't offend; let's be quiet; let's keep it played down!

The Bible contains much that is offensive to the intellectual, yet God has called us to a whole-hearted commitment to his truth, to the cross, to the outpouring of the Spirit, to the church coming to fullness of stature.

In Gideon's day, when they gave themselves to the worship of other gods, God's prophetic word to them was, 'I will not own you until you put these things right.' It is also his word to us today. God will never say 'If they can't do what I require I will drop the standards and bless them.' He will simply wait for another generation. This does not prove that God is weak. He is not thrown if someone scrawls on the wall: 'God is dead,' because he sits a king for ever! We can get anxious about it, but Jesus is King and, if necessary, he will wait for another generation. God will have a people who live according to his standard, that he might display them for his glory and honour.

## Embrace the cross

God wants us to be free from this world. How do we get free? There is only one way and that is through the cross of our Lord Jesus Christ. The apostle Paul said, 'May it never be that I should boast, except in the cross of our Lord Jesus Christ' (Gal 6:14). He did not say, 'I boast in the memory of it.' He did not even say, 'I boast in the cross as I consider what Jesus did for me.' He said, 'May it never be that I should boast except in the cross of our Lord Jesus Christ, through which the world has been crucified to me, and I to the world.' He gloried in it experientially. He said, in effect, 'This cross has released me from the world. It has delivered me from the gods all around me. I now live to God as one alive from the dead.'

The cross is not something to glory in as a memory. It is a mighty, powerful instrument in our lives that sets us free. Through it we died to these gods in order that we might rise up holy, free and pure.

Is that the way you are living?

God's prophetic word to us today is exactly the same as it was in the days of the Judges. He is saying, 'I am your covenant God. I brought you out of Egypt, but you are worshipping other gods. You make your decisions before them and not before me.' As in the book of Revelation, Jesus says to us, 'I have this against you.' Prophet after prophet in the Old Testament thundered out this word. They spoke continually against compromise. Elijah said, 'How long will you hesitate between two opinions? If the Lord is God, follow Him' (1 Kings 18:21).

If we will hear this word now, and respond as Gideon did, then God will move once more. It only needs a small company to obey at first. God said in Isaiah that the increase of his government will be 'as at the battle of Midian' (9:4). That was a time when a small company of people heard the prophet, followed anointed leadership and committed themselves to the army. That is all that God needs. That is all he is waiting for. Then he can turn the land upside down.

We don't need to pray about the Midianites and their camels, or whatever their modern equivalents might be. We need to respond to the prophetic word and God will turn our land upside down.

## 10

# *Finding the Right Man*

Following the prophet's word, God, in his great mercy, began to provide his answer. First he sent an angel. It is particularly interesting to note that God did not send his angel to rout the Midianites but to speak to a man.

An angel may be empowered to do great and mighty things, but God has committed his purpose to men and does not ultimately bypass them. However black the situation is, God does not say, 'I will have to work by my angel power this time.' In these days of spiritual darkness, God is still looking for men he can work through.

We read that the angel sent to Gideon was actually 'the angel of the Lord'. The same 'angel of the Lord' who appeared to Joshua and Abraham—the pre-incarnate Lord Jesus—found Gideon. The angel of the Lord whose mere breath could have destroyed Midian unaided was selecting his chosen instrument.

In John 15:5 Jesus says, 'I am the vine, you are the branches...apart from Me you can do nothing.' The amazing implication of this is that he is also saying that since we are his branches he does nothing without us. Not because he lacks sovereign power, but because he has chosen to accomplish his purposes on earth through the people he loves.

**What kind of man?**

One might imagine that God would seek out a powerful, dynamic leader from among his people. It was, after all, a fairly hopeless situation. The Israelites were living a beggarly existence, hiding in caves and threatened always by savage Midianite raids. God, one might expect, would be looking for an identifiable national hero, a focus for his people's aspirations; ideally, someone strong, courageous, persuasive, influential, clear-sighted and determined.

But the angel of the Lord found Gideon. Was it a joke, or had he made a mistake? Did he not know, Gideon wondered, that he had just approached the least significant member of the least significant family of the least significant tribe in all Israel? Gideon was a nobody, so why was he chosen of all people?

We, however, should be less surprised at God's choice than Gideon was. The Scriptures teach us that very often God calls the young, the unqualified and the inexperienced into his service.

When God sent Samuel to Jesse's household to anoint the future king, Samuel met many tall, good looking, accomplished young men, but God kept saying 'no', until the youngest appeared. This was the young boy, David, who had been out in the field looking after a few sheep. Nobody had considered him, but he was God's choice. The youngest, the least.

Similarly, we read that Jeremiah considered himself too young. The apostle Paul had to encourage Timothy not to let men despise his youth. Joseph and David were both young men when God laid hold of their lives and so, of course, was Samuel.

Gideon, however, was different from other young men that God called. Whereas the others had much to commend them, Gideon did not. David may have been young and inexperienced, but he had killed a lion and fought a bear. He knew and loved God, and worshipped him with his harp. Although he was young, he was full of zeal and faith and was unafraid to face Goliath.

Daniel also may have been young, but he was a man of integrity and clarity, a man of determined purpose. They both had things to commend them but Gideon seemed to have nothing to commend him at all. Not only was he insignificant, he was totally insecure.

## The feeblest saint

Joseph, as a young man, saw visions—Gideon only saw problems! He was just a feeble, insecure man. Look at the way he responded to the call of God. He said, 'If it is you speaking to me, I'll just go and prepare something for you.' So he prepared a meal and put it on the rock. The angel of the Lord then touched it with his rod and it vanished in smoke, whereupon the angel also disappeared. Any of *us* would have thought, 'That clinches it, it really is God!' But, no, that was not enough for Gideon.

Later on, even after God had been speaking to him so clearly, we find the strange story with the fleece. He asked God to confirm his intentions once more by a miraculous sign. If the fleece he left overnight was wet with dew and the ground was bone dry, then he would know for sure. When he woke up the next morning and God had answered his prayer, even that was not enough. Still insecure, still uncertain, he reversed the sequence—'Let the rain be here and let it be dry there.' Never satisfied!

Finally, just before the battle God said to Gideon, 'You are still frightened, so go down and listen to the enemy.' With every sign from God rejected, Gideon then had to hear the truth from the lips of his enemies. He overheard his victory foretold in a dream, and at last Gideon believed. This is the man God chose! God's man of faith and power? You would have expected God to find somebody quite different, but he actually used the weakest and the most insignificant man.

How often we say, 'If only God would convert some-body in a position of political power. If only that TV personality, pop singer or footballer could come for-ward—then we could hear his testimony and hundreds of teenagers would sweep in.' But the Scripture says again and again—God chooses whom he will!

Have a look in 1 Corinthians 1:26–29,

> For consider your calling, brethren, that there were not many wise according to the flesh, not many mighty, not many noble; but God has chosen the foolish things of the world to shame the wise, and God has chosen the weak things of the world to shame the things which are strong, and the base things of the world and the despised, God has chosen, the things that are not, that He might nullify the things that are, that no man should boast before God.

So often we point to factors which we think disqualify us, when they are the very things that God is looking for! God sees us feeling so weak, but God has chosen the weak. We say, 'I am hopeless, I am despised.' God says, 'That's exactly what I want. In this time of spiritual black-ness, I want to do a very great thing and I must find weak people.' Often the problem that God has with us is that we are too strong. We have too much to offer, while he is looking for vulnerable people. Blessed are the poor in spirit, for theirs is the kingdom of heaven.

## Mighty man of valour

When God called Gideon a 'mighty man of valour', it must have been one of the best jokes since Abram was renamed Abraham. Abram had suffered the indignity of a totally inappropriate name, which means 'exalted father'! He had struggled hard to live up to that name and God had to make it even worse! He renamed him Abraham—

'father of a multitude'. Abram was bad enough, but why Abraham? Nevertheless, we find that when God speaks, miracles are accomplished. Abraham eventually became what God called him. When God speaks, he calls things that are not as though they were. God created the heavens and the earth out of nothing, by the word of his power. He spoke, and they sprang into being. And God would speak to us: 'If any man is in Christ, he is a new creature; the old things passed away; behold, new things have come' (2 Cor 5:17). He speaks and it is done. He said to Simon Peter, fully aware of all his weaknesses: 'Simon, son of Jonah, you shall be Peter.' Jesus spoke and this unstable man eventually became rock-like, living up to his new name.

The man that God called 'a mighty man of valour' was, however, at that point, still full of fear and insecurity. We may assume that he was also hurt because he said, 'The Lord has abandoned us'—which was not true. God will sometimes put us through very difficult times, allowing great pressures to come upon us to bring us into maturity, but he never, never abandons us. Yet Gideon said, 'The Lord has abandoned us.' He was a wounded man as well as a weak man and yet God chose him.

He said, 'There's one weak enough who won't be proud in my hands, one I can work through'. No one is disqualified. God can pick up the frailest and use them.

## Where are the miracles?

It would be wrong, however, to think that Gideon had nothing going for him. If he had no other strengths, he was a man thirsty for God. When the angel of the Lord addressed him, he at least cared about the glory of God and the state of the nation. His response may have been weak, but at least it revealed how he felt about Israel's situation, and how in his heart he longed for God to manifest his power. The angel's appearance provoked a torrent of questions: 'Why has all this happened? Where are the wonders that our fathers spoke of when they told us that God rescued us from Egypt?' In all his weakness he was hungry for God.

How is it with you? Do you ask, 'Lord, why is it like this—why is your church so small? Where are all the miracles? Where is the great turning to you? Where is the demonstration that Jesus is alive?'

When Paul came to Athens and saw all the idolatry, his spirit was provoked within him. Are our spirits provoked within us, or have we come to settle? There must have been dispensationalists in Gideon's day. They probably said that it was in the 'Joshua dispensation' that rivers opened up and walls fell down! 'Now, you have to understand that was all in the past. That was just to get us into the land, just to get things going. Now we don't need miracles, now we are in the land—in hiding, yes, but we are in!'

Some of us have been raised on such teaching. The power, the glory and the gifts of the Spirit were just to get the church started. Now we have come to maturity, it is argued, we do not need those things. But Gideon rejected such notions and longed for God's power to be seen. God looks for people like that—however weak they are. God does not despise your weakness, but he looks for soul thirst. He is not merely looking for those who know all the jargon, because commitment and obedience in themselves can be cold and routine. The people God delights in are those who cry out in their spirits, 'I am hungry for God and I long to see him.'

Moses said, 'If I have found favor in Thy sight, let me know Thy ways' (Exod 33:13). He was so hungry for God that even at the end of his life he said, 'O God, you have only just begun to show me your greatness.' He had an appetite for God himself. He did not just say, 'Thank goodness I've found grace—let's sing some choruses about grace.' He saw that if he was in grace and that God was going to love him in spite of all his shortcomings, then perhaps God would reveal more of himself. Although he had to carry the whole nation, he still had time to get before God and say, 'O God, show me your glory.' His desire was for God. His continual prayer was, 'Let me see more of you, you are so wonderful. I am not content just leading your flock through the wilderness to the promised land. I am not content merely to see your great programme for them—I want to know you.' God delights in people like that, who are not just interested in what is happening in the church at large, but are saying, 'O God, I have a personal appetite for you.'

Jacob, similarly, with all his weaknesses and faults, nonetheless had an appetite for God. He was a crook, but he wanted God and God loved him and drew him on.

We, as Christians at the close of the twentieth century, are in great danger of superficiality, routinely 'doing the Lord's work' for no better reason than 'there's work to be done'. God desires a warmer relationship than that. Peter had many weaknesses, but he could say, 'Lord, I have left everything to follow you.' Can we say that?

We read of Nehemiah that when he heard about the situation in Jerusalem, his heart was overwhelmed with grief. Jerusalem's walls were in ruins and he wept and cried to God because he was zealous for Zion, zealous for the house of God.

God would have us to be such a people. Although we are weak and although we are frail, we are to be a people who are zealous for his house and who want to see the power of God manifest. This is the only qualification I can see in this man Gideon to start with—he had a hunger to see God at work.

Do you have a hunger to see God at work once more in power and glory? Or will you settle with the view that these are just quiet days for the church—days to muddle through somehow, to survive, to hope for the best? Gideon was weak, but longed for God!

# 11

# *Sent by God*

If weakness and spiritual hunger prepared Gideon for
God's service, we must learn from this story that there
was a third, more important, qualification. He became a
man *sent and commissioned by God*. He heard God say:
'The Lord is with you. Go in this your strength and deliver
Israel. Have not I sent you? Surely I will be with you.'

A man who hears things like that from God has nothing
to fear. A man who has heard that kind of promise has all
heaven behind him. God's purpose must be established
through such a person because his actions are not rooted
merely in his own ideas. He is not simply responding to
the need. He is not just saying, 'I am not going to put up
with this any more. I am going to go out after those
Midianites'—not a mere man moving on his own initiative.
He has heard from God. God has laid hold of him. God
will not necessarily own our activities but, if he has sent
us, we have his guarantee that he will own us as we do his
bidding.

## The need and the call

Some say, 'The need constitutes the call. Because the
mission field waits, we must go.' But Jesus did not say,
'Look, the harvest fields are white to harvest—*go*, there-

fore.' He said, 'The fields are white unto harvest. *Pray*
therefore that the Lord of the harvest shall send forth his
labourers—thrust them forth' (see Mt 9:38; Jn 4:35).
There is all the difference in the world between a man who
sees the need and rushes into it wondering if God is with
him, and the man who, perhaps even reluctantly, has
heard the call of God and goes, knowing that God's hand
is upon him.

Look at Moses! As a young and powerful prince in
Egypt he saw a great need. His own people were
oppressed and suffering in slavery and so he rushed in and
slew an Egyptian. His best intentions went horribly wrong
and he ended up having to flee. Why? *Because God did
not send him.* Later on God said, '*I have come down to
deliver them and, behold, I now send you.*' This was a
different situation altogether. The same man was involved, but this time he was not rushing in to do what he
could. God said, 'I have seen the need and now I am
sending you. I am the one who is doing the delivering.'
That is how it had to be with Gideon. 'I know your
weakness,' God said, 'but I have sent you; therefore, I am
going to do it.' It is never enough for us to say: 'The need
is there. We must rush to the need. We must answer the
need,' and hope that God agrees. We must hear what he
says. The question arises, 'Will they hear without a
preacher?', but another question follows on its
heels—'How will they go unless they are sent?'

When Paul's vision led him to Macedonia, he ended up
in prison. If he had not known in his heart that God had
sent him, the situation would have been devastating! As it
was, he was full of praise and rejoicing because, although
his circumstances were dreadful, he knew he was right on
course. Similarly, we sometimes find ourselves dogged by
difficulties and pressures, but if we know we are where
God has called us to be, then we can also rejoice. No
matter how difficult our circumstances appear, we can be
at rest if we know that God has sent us.

I remember when I first heard a missionary appeal:

'Young men are needed on the mission field. Who will go?
The music played and all the women walked down the
aisle! The preacher said, 'Where are all the men who will
go?' I remember thinking, 'Yes, of course, they need
somebody like me. Someone who will sort out a few
things, get rid of some of the old-fashioned ways, introduce some modern ideas. Here I am—just as I am—
young, strong and free to be the best that I can be!' When,
however, the young Moses volunteered like that, God
accepted him, but spent forty years preparing him in the
wilderness!

Gideon did not emerge as one 'young, strong and free'!
Gideon came in all his weakness, but God apprehended
him. He did not take it upon himself to do God's work
simply because he was free and able. He went because
God sent him.

Bob Mumford says, 'God has more problems with those
who want to help him than he has with backsliders!' We
must wait for God to speak to us. The Israelites were
under the Midianite yoke because of the very judgement
of God. We must move in the fear of God. If we blindly
rush in, however good our intentions might be, there
always remains the possibility that we could actually be
opposing the will of God. We must wait for him to speak
and then, when he does, he will transform us into a people
of faith.


## By faith

And it is to this aspect of faith that we must now turn our
attention. Gideon was once timid, fearful and weak, but
through the call of God he was transformed into a man of
real faith. It is scarcely believable, yet Gideon finally
appears in the Bible in Hebrews 11—that great chapter of
faith. One is tempted to ask, 'How on earth did he get
there?' Gideon of all people! Time did not permit the
writer to the Hebrews to go into detail about all those

listed, but if we glance through that famous chapter to verse 34, we read of one who by faith 'from weakness [was] made strong, became mighty in war, put foreign armies to flight'. Gideon, by faith, became strong out of weakness and qualified for Hebrews 11.

God sees you in your weakness and says, 'O mighty man of valour, I'll get you into Hebrews 11! I'll get you into my book of heroes! I know what I can do with you in all your frailty.' Hallelujah! It thrills my heart. God can say that to any one of us in all our weakness.

We must become men and women of faith. There is no other way, no bypass. It is nonsense to say, 'I am too weak to become a man of faith.' God doesn't despise your weakness, but he will not bless your unbelief. It is never enough merely to hear God's voice if we do not fully trust him. Without faith it is impossible to please him! We must not hide behind our weaknesses, because when God says, 'I have called you, and now I send you,' everything changes. You can become a person of real faith. But if you do not respond to his word, if you continue to doubt and do not grow in faith, you will fail to do the work God has called you to. The battle ahead for Gideon was going to be a battle of faith. The Israelites were not merely outnumbered, but faced ridiculous, impossible odds. The battle demanded faith, and today's battles are no different. The whole Christian life is lived by faith.

If we do not respond in faith to God, we shall forever limit our activities to the things we can do in our natural strength. We argue, 'This is something I *know* I can do,' and, as a result, fail to live by faith beyond our previous limitations. But God says the just shall live by faith and, inevitably, there will be times when he asks us to do things totally beyond our natural ability—things which we simply feel we cannot do! It might be leading in prayer, giving our testimony in public, or door-to-door evangelism. The immediate response might well be like Gideon's: 'You know me, I couldn't possibly do that!' But we will hold back God's work if we continue to live only within the restricted sphere of our own ability.

The rot sets in if we respond to God's promptings with self-doubt. Too often we evaluate fresh challenges by reference to our previous experience, our education, our personality, strength and ability. But God says, 'By faith I want you to step right out of this. By faith come right out of your limitation.' We will never turn the world upside down unless we begin living by faith.

God says, 'Do not fear, you worm Jacob...I have made you a new, sharp threshing sledge with double edges; you will thresh the mountains' (Is 41:14). We do not have to stay as worms all the time. We must believe whole-heartedly and move beyond our previous limitations. Gideon became a man of faith and, even though it was with some trembling, he followed God. When God told him to destroy the altar of Baal, Gideon obeyed secretly and at night, supported by friends—but he did it! God prefers trembling obedience to bravado that has not even counted the cost.

We all respond with faith at the time of our conversion, but God wants us to live by faith all the time.

## Steps of faith

Some years ago, when I was a commuter, I had a friend who went through every compartment on the Brighton to Victoria train giving out tracts. This, as you can imagine, is not a formula for popularity among slumbering or news-paper-reading commuters—but he did it. The incident brought me into complete condemnation because I knew it was something that I would never have the courage to do. However, some time later God said to me very clearly, 'I want you to testify to the people in your com-partment and give them tracts!' I said, 'Lord, I can't do that.' But God had been showing me that I had to venture into situations beyond my own ability. He spoke to me from the story of Joshua where it says that when their feet actually touched the River Jordan, it opened. When they actually stepped into it, God acted.

In all probability I would have stood all day by the River Jordan. I may have even arranged nights of prayer and fasting as well, but as for putting my foot into the water before it opened—well, that would be scary! Many of us would have said, 'O Lord, I'll pray all night!', but God said, 'Put your foot in the water!' God says, 'Move out of your areas of ability into my areas of ability. Let's see what I can do.'

So God said to me, 'You give out tracts in your compartment.' I said, 'Lord, I can't do that, but what I can do is put the tracts in my pocket. That's as far as I can go.' It was my way of putting my feet in the water, as it were. So I put the tracts in my pocket and I sat there on the train going from Brighton to London. When we got to Vauxhall Bridge (which is a fair way on!) I finally *found myself* (I choose those words) taking them out of my pocket. I found myself saying to the people in that compartment, 'These are about Jesus. I would like you to read them as he has done so much for me.' Afterwards, I sat there amazed. I suddenly found I could do the thing that I thought I could not do—and for me it was a miracle!

Many of us limit what God is able to do simply by denying him the opportunity to work. We flatly state, 'I can't do that,' and effectively prevent him from showing his power.

Gideon became strong by faith, and if God can make a man like Gideon a man of faith, he can do it for anyone. He will not bless unbelief. He loves even the faintest glimmer of genuine faith.

## Trust and obey

The next thing we must learn about Gideon is that he was a man of obedience to God. In all his weakness, he was obedient. God said, 'Gideon, the first thing you have got to do is pull down that altar in your own home.' He was obedient to God at home base first of all. One of the vital things God is showing us today is that our obedience must first be demonstrated at this private level. Later on, Gideon will stand up in battle and cry out, 'Do as I do.' Leaders must face the responsibility of saying, 'Look at me and do likewise.' So God warned Gideon, 'Before I get you into such a place, I have something to say to you about your home and the other god that is being worshipped there. Pull it down!' Any man or woman who is going to be used by God must get to grips with anything that is spoiling their life or home.

Maybe it will be costly. It was costly for Gideon—he risked the wrath of his father and of the city—but God said, 'This is between you and me, Gideon. Do it.' Therefore, in all his weakness, together with a few friends around him, he obeyed God. He put himself in danger with those who were closest to him.

In Luke 12, Jesus said some words that he has never taken back from his commission to his church:

> Do you suppose that I came to grant peace on earth? I tell you, no, but rather division; for from now on five members in one household will be divided, three against two, and two against three. They will be divided, father against son and son against father; mother against daughter and daughter against mother; mother-in-law against daughter-in-law, and daughter-in-law against mother-in-law (vv. 51–53).

If you are going to take this whole move of the Spirit seriously, what will your family say? How will friends at church react if they hear you have embraced this 'tongues thing'? Will you press on after God? Is it in your heart to obey him, however painful? God would say to us, 'Will you go on with me whatever it costs? No matter how weak, insecure and wounded you are, I can use you if you are obedient.'

If you will obey God in your home and in your private world, God will bless and own you and develop his purpose in you. It could be that you will need help. You may need friends to stand with you as Gideon did. But you must pull down all that offends God in your home life, whatever the cost. This cannot be bypassed no matter how tempting it is to try. The Lord will not own the man who says, 'I'll be a leader but don't look too closely at my home.' The altar to Baal must go first—and then see what God can do.

## Peace with God

Gideon's quiet lifestyle was being revolutionized by this devastating encounter with God. Nevertheless, God loved him and had great plans for him and so he spoke peace into his heart. He gave him a new revelation—Jehovah Shalom—God is peace. We too must know this revelation. We need to know that God has taken away all our condemnation. God has dealt with the fear that comes upon us when we suddenly realize that we are dealing with God. When Gideon knew it was God, he felt condemned. But God said, 'Do not fear, you shall not die. I am the God who sends peace.' Being justified by faith, you have peace with God. You cannot serve God unless you have peace with him. It is futile trying to serve him to prove yourself to him, hoping that in some way perhaps you will improve in his estimation. He is Jehovah Shalom. He gives you peace on the ground of his covenant relationship with you. He *gives* peace by his grace.

Gideon came to understand that God had accepted him and received him as he was. Gideon experienced this beautiful revelation—Jehovah Shalom—the Lord gives peace. Do you know God's peace as you serve him? It is so important to understand that we do not work for him in the hope that he will eventually accept us. To believe that would be to live always in condemnation. Whether you succeed or fail, nonetheless the Lord gives peace. This peace is unconditionally yours on the grounds of his grace relationship with you!

## Clothed with power

Finally, we read in Judges 6:34 that the Spirit of the Lord came upon him, equipping him for the task. God's timing was perfect because Gideon came to faith and was filled with the Spirit at the very same time that the Midianites began to move in. They would raid, it seems, whenever they felt there was something worth destroying. As soon as the Israelites began to re-establish themselves, as soon as the fields began to produce again, the sons of the East would appear. The vast Midianite army would fill the horizon, sinking terror into the hearts of God's people. But this time there was a man who had come to faith. Gideon, newly filled with the Spirit, came face to face with the real issue. This time, the impossible was confronted by faith.

When the Virgin Mary was faced with the impossible as the angel told her of what was to come, she asked, 'How can this be?' God's answer was, 'The Spirit of the Lord shall come upon you.' Similarly, when Gideon saw the huge armies assembling in the distance he might have asked, 'How is this going to work?' But God's solution has always been the same. The Spirit of the Lord 'clothed' Gideon, or should we say, 'clothed himself with' Gideon. The result was a changed man—a man of power by the Spirit.

You shall receive power when the Holy Spirit comes upon you, the Scripture promises. That is God's answer in these dark days as he begins to stir us and kindle us. The wind is blowing upon the dry bones. The Spirit of God is coming upon us in power and glory. The Holy Spirit is changing us, transforming us, giving us ability that we never had before; releasing us from our fears, bringing us into freedom and power by his grace. Have you received the Holy Spirit since you believed? Have you been clothed with that power?

Today, we are living in an age of the Spirit. We are living in days when God says, 'I will pour out my Spirit—not on the occasional leader like Gideon; not on the occasional judge or king. I will pour out my Spirit on all flesh. Your sons and your daughters shall prophesy, your old men will dream dreams, your young men shall see visions.' God is pouring out his Spirit—and every one of us can be filled by him to move into the battle.

The coming of the light of the kingdom will be like the battle of Midian. Be sure you are prepared.

# 12

# *A Committed Army*

As we have already seen in chapter 2, when God breaks powerfully into a situation, it is often possible to observe a distinct pattern of events. First comes a prophetic explanation; secondly, God chooses and anoints leadership—in this case Gideon—then, thirdly, God calls together a committed army. Now we must turn to see what kind of army God uses because *we* are that army and Christ, not Gideon, is our Captain. Today God is raising an army throughout the nations which is destined to be the most significant army the world has ever seen.

## An army with faith

The first thing about Gideon's army was that it was an army which had faith. Not only was their leader a man of faith—each one had to have his own faith. The first command given was: 'Let all who are fearful go home.' That command was not unique to this battle (see Deut 20:8), but it was doubly necessary on this occasion when they were so outnumbered. If you can imagine this little company looking down the valley at the vast Midianite army and their camels, it is no wonder that Gideon needed a fearless army! Twenty-two thousand went home, so the steadfast who remained were not fearful, but men of faith.

Faith is the very opposite of fear. You cannot experience both at the same time. Jesus directed, 'Fear not, only believe.' God wants a people whose faith overcomes their fear. Often, when preachers call us to greater commitment, we find a question rising in our hearts: 'But what if . . . ?' Three small words born of fear. What will be the repercussions if I do this? How will I be thought of at home? What will they say? We persist in asking these questions while the Scriptures warn us that fear can steal so much of our inheritance.

When the Pharisees confronted Jesus regarding his authority he answered them with another question. He asked by what authority John baptized people. The Pharisees did not answer immediately, but began to weigh up the implications of their answers. If they had said, 'By God's authority,' Jesus could have asked, 'Why then were you not baptized? If they had said that John was not from God, they knew they would incur the wrath of the people, who commonly held John to be a prophet. So they said, 'We do not know!' Rather than answer honestly, they ducked a question that was too hot to handle!

In a similar fashion, some of us hear the word of God and weigh up the repercussions of what we are hearing. We say, 'If I follow this, if I do that, such-and-such will happen.' We might agree with the preacher, but we are not ready for the implications. We weigh up the possible repercussions of our alternative responses and end up robbed by fear. The preaching moves us deeply time and time again, but we persist in saying, 'I don't really know— I'm not sure.'

Many went to hear John the Baptist preach—even the king went occasionally—just to witness the charisma of the mighty prophet. Ezekiel spoke the word of God to vast crowds, but to them he was 'nothing more than one who sings love songs with a beautiful voice and plays an instrument well' (Ezek 33:32, NIV). But what does one who plays an instrument well accomplish? He thrills his audience with skilful playing and they praise the skill displayed, just as the singer of love songs moves hearts. But that is all. For a few moments people are moved—but not changed!

God wants us to be released from fear and to embrace his purposes. We must not think that Christianity is only for the naturally courageous, any more than it is only for the naturally brilliant. We know that God is for the smallest child, so commitment is not only for the naturally tough guys! The naturally timid must not assume they have no chance and might as well go home. If that were so, then Gideon should have led the way as he was one of the most fearful there.

Instead, the story shows us that God can apprehend the naturally timid and transform them. The church does not consist of only the courageous. It is for those who will respond to God and become strong, like Gideon, whether they are leaders or not. When God was looking for a young man to lead Israel through the River Jordan into the promised land, he did not advertise in the *Wilderness Times*: 'Wanted! Young man good at walking through rivers.' If he had, he should have added, 'No previous experience required'!

## An army with courage

The church must become more bold. Most of us have grown up in times where believers do not require much courage. But, historically, whenever God has moved with power there has always been a price to pay. As the church gathers her strength and becomes a force in the world, there is always a backlash.

To date, the majority of us have only experienced occasional mocking. Others have experienced a form of persecution from their own brothers in Christ over one matter or another. But as the church grows and society begins to be affected by the power of the gospel, real persecution will ensue.

I had to fill in an insurance form recently, on which was asked my occupation. I wrote 'Christian minister', and was then faced with the question, 'Are there any special dangers attached to your job?' I felt like answering, 'Not yet!' The man in the street might well scoff at the notion of a minister of religion being engaged in a dangerous occupation, but imagine the Apostle Paul filling in the same form! What a catalogue of beatings, imprisonments, shipwrecks and attempted murders he would have to record. We must never forget that we follow a leader who was crucified! When the church arises in power, threatening world forces and challenging the darkness, a backlash will occur. The battle will require faith and courage. Let us recognize this now and become that army of faith.

## An obedient army

The next thing about this army was that it was an obedient army which was clearly demonstrated by their willingness to follow their leader. The old hymn tells us:

> Trust and obey
> For there's no other way
> To be happy in Jesus
> Than to trust and obey.

Few would question the importance of obedience in the Christian walk. At the same time, we evangelicals have strongly emphasized the *personal* nature of our faith, thus providing plenty of scope for the individual to actually be independent, wayward and even self-willed. These soldiers demonstrated their obedience to God by obeying their God-given leader.

Obedience, one might argue, would be easy if our leaders were always like David or Daniel. They were obviously valiant, faithful leaders. But what about Gideon? Following that weak, unremarkable man from the smallest of the tribes must have presented quite a challenge! But the Lord chose Gideon, put his Spirit upon him and appointed him to lead. By obeying the one whom God has chosen, called and anointed, that army was obeying God. And this pinpoints one of the great truths that God is restoring to his church in these days: leaders must be free to lead.

For too long now the church has been weakened by individualism. Many could almost sing with Frank Sinatra, 'I did it my way.' Adam could have sung that as he walked out of the garden. So could Saul as he lost the kingdom. But sin is rooted in 'doing it our way'. Isaiah tells us, 'Each of us has turned to his own way; but the Lord has caused the iniquity of us all to fall on Him.' We charismatics are particularly vulnerable, because now we claim to receive 'revelations'. 'The Lord told me...' can often be independence masquerading as spirituality. Such practice will bring us onto dangerous ground unless we build in the safeguards provided by godly leadership which Christ has ordained for his church. Certainly we can all hear personally from God—that is an integral part of our inheritance as Christians—but God has also seen our need for mature oversight in the church.

Many years ago my wife and I borrowed a washing machine and the instructions said, 'Before use, secure this to the ground.' Since we were only borrowing it for a while, we did not bother. We filled it and turned it on, and it chased us round the kitchen! Undisciplined power can create havoc! For some twenty years now, God has graciously been pouring out his Spirit on thirsty people. Now he is looking for his army to arise. This means learning the lesson of manifest obedience, not just 'the Lord and me'.

### Sub-divided for action

Gideon divided his men into three groups. No one is

recorded as saying, 'But I liked it when we were all one.'
Gideon said, 'We are going to be in three sections from
now on.' He did not invite a vote about it. There is no
record that he asked the soldiers which groups they would
like to be in. Gideon placed them. We must take note of
this, particularly as God is leading many to divide their
churches into congregations, cells and home groups. At
such times we find whether we have the qualities of this
army or not. Will we go where we are asked to go or reply,
'I don't like that group. I would rather be in this one.'
Some might have been tempted to say, 'I want to be with
you, Gideon. You are the man of God.' But God often
puts us into situations, not just for our immediate blessing,
but also for our long-term training.

Joseph was in a lovely 'home group' at the beginning—
his father's. Then he found himself moved into Potiphar's
'house group' and he blessed the house. Where he went
there was blessing. Then he was transferred from Potiphar's 'house group' to the 'prison group', and he blessed
the prison. In the end he was such a blessing in the prison
that he was given more responsibility. He finally finished
up with a group of his own—and quite a large one!

Those of you who are jostling for position, are you
willing to abandon your personal preferences and say,
'Lord, I will stay here and learn from you through this
situation. I believe you are teaching me your ways'?

Jesus often trained his disciples in that kind of way. He
asked them to do things that seemed foolish, such as
casting the net on the other side of the boat. They had
been fishing all night, but Jesus said, 'Fish on the other
side,' and they did. Then at Cana when they ran out of
wine, he said, 'Go and fill the jars with water,' and they
did. When they had to pay taxes, Jesus said, 'Go and catch
a fish—you will find a coin there.'

What was he doing? He was training this little group to
do whatever he said, unswervingly and without question.
Gradually, he fashioned those men. He sent them on all

kinds of peculiar errands which in themselves had no great significance, except that he was teaching them to do things simply because he said so.

If we are to become an army that will turn the world upside-down, we have to learn the same lessons. A leader does not want to have to explain his every decision or for ever have to coax his people to embrace the vision that God has shown him. Gideon said, 'Watch me and what I do, then do likewise.' This is one of the hallmarks of anointed leadership. It was not simply a matter of getting others to do things for him, but rather Gideon led by example.

Another sign of an authentic leader is that God blesses his activities. If, when Jesus had given his commands, the water had not turned into wine or there had not been a coin in the mouth of the fish, then his followers really would have needed to ask some questions. Real leaders (while they may sometimes get things wrong) are not for ever leading us on ventures that do not work or up blind alleys. If they do, we can question their calling to leadership. On the contrary, with a real leader you can sense that God is with him and you want to be in his slipstream just to see what God will do next.

Can I ask you—do you recognize yourself in this army yet? Are you in a position where a God-given leader can count on your commitment? Have you said to anybody, 'I want to join you. I feel that God has raised you up, given you leadership ability and I want to be committed here'? Are you with leadership that knows where it is going or are you in a situation that is going nowhere?

All around us sinners are 'sitting in darkness and the shadow of death', while the church remains ineffective. Thousands are dying daily without Christ, while the church goes round in ineffectual circles. May God help us to gird ourselves for action and find our place in his army—an army with faith, courage and discipline!

# 13

## *Using the Right Weapons*

How did this extraordinary army transform apparent defeat into total victory? By using powerful weapons! Yet the weapons they employed were non-material and totally spiritual. Although they were instructed to shout, 'A sword for the Lord and for Gideon' (Judg 7:20), they did not have one sword between them! They went out with pitchers and lights and trumpets, but no swords. 'The weapons of our warfare,' Paul wrote, 'are not of the flesh, but divinely powerful' (2 Cor 10:4).

The first significant weapon they used in the battle can easily be overlooked. It was in fact their *unity*. You might expect me to interpret the spiritual significance of the trumpet, the pitcher and the light. They had to break their pitchers, and let their lights shine. We might argue, 'Isn't the lesson all about the breaking of our outer man to let God's light shine through?' Personally, I do not believe that is the heart of the matter at all. Imagine if one individual had embraced the truth regarding the need for 'brokenness', broken his vessel, held up his light and blown his trumpet on his own. The result would have been total failure. The weapons had no value in themselves at all! Their success depended on them all acting together. The power of their strategy was unity—that was their spiritual weapon—they all acted as one man! Without united action those weapons would never work. Charismatics must hear this! Without unity, the weapons God is putting in our hands will never work. The spiritual weapon they used was unity. They would have been a total disaster if they had not been absolutely and entirely together in what they were doing.

We must all be committed and loyal to one another, for where there is unity God will command blessing. It is easy to feel loyal and united at large Christian conventions where we come and worship together. People embrace, laugh, enjoy good fellowship and sing, 'Bind us together, Lord.' In that lovely setting we feel a tremendous sense of oneness. But real unity is seldom tested there. The tests start when we have all gone our separate ways. Real unity is challenged when we begin to hear rumours about one another.

Rumours breed fears and anxieties which become suspicions that take form and are then passed on as fact. Gradually, a catalogue of hurt, mistrust and bitterness is inflicted on God's people. True unity, however, develops a heart attitude that will refuse to believe rumours without checking them out. Where there is unity, rumours will not even be allowed to colour our thinking towards a brother. Christians should not even accept unproven rumours concerning their enemies. How much more should they be diligent to work out brotherly loyalty to their fellow believers. Rumour and hearsay are to be totally rejected by the people of God.

I wonder if you have ever been to a party where everyone sits in a circle and someone whispers a message in the ear of their neighbour who in turn whispers to the next until the message arrives at the end of the circle. Usually it bears little resemblance to the original. Imagine Gideon's group of 300 encircling the valley containing the Midianites.

The darkness of the night separates them from one another as they take up their positions. A tiny army of 300 looks down on the Midianite hordes. Try to imagine the scene. After what seems like an endless delay, waiting for the cry of command, one calls out to his nearest neighbour through the darkness, 'What was it we had to shout?'

'A sword for the Lord and for Gideon!' comes the reply. 'Pass it on.'

The next enquires, 'What was the cry?'

'Something about Gideon's sword,' comes the answer.

After a few more exchanges, the message becomes, 'Gideon has a sword,' until suddenly one frightened and disgruntled soldier sees a terrible injustice here.

'Did you say that Gideon had a sword? Why haven't I got a sword? Gideon certainly looked after himself, didn't he? All we have is a light, a pitcher and a trumpet, and Gideon has a sword...!'

A farcical scene, but things not unlike that happen in the church of God. Rumours are not checked out, suspicions are passed on as facts, often chaos prevails. We must fear God and be steadfast and loyal to our brothers. I am labouring the point, but lack of unity is frustrating the work of God—it has been for years! Will you refuse to accept rumours until you have checked them out and know the truth of the matter? Gideon's men remained united even under pressure, even separated in the darkness!

Paul called the Colossians to put on a heart of compassion, kindness, humility, gentleness and patience, and to bear with one another and to forgive just as they had been forgiven. He reminded them that God had commanded his chosen people to put on love, which is the perfect bond of unity, and to let Christ rule in their hearts. If we forget that we are members of one another, we shall never be united, and without unity we shall never become an effective army.

## Having strategy

The second powerful spiritual weapon deployed at the battle of Gideon was divine strategy. Each one stood in his place. The ruse required that these men should give the appearance of a vast army. They had to be properly staggered around the hillside. Each light, each trumpet and each shout, had to make a contribution by virtue of their being in exactly the right place.

Imagine Gideon's soldiers finding their places around the hillside. One sees an elderly lady struggling with a heavy load of provisions and offers her help. Another hears a little boy lost in a cave and goes to find him. These distractions, however worthy in themselves, would have been totally in conflict with God's strategy for that moment. It would have cost them the battle.

Is your light shining where God wants it to? He wants us in the place of maximum impact. We are not meant to be stumbling upon random 'good causes'. Each of us has significance in our own right and is ultimately going to give an account of what we have done with our light. We are not driftwood; we are meant to be standing in the best possible place to count for God.

## Playing your part

Thirdly, Gideon's soldiers were not only standing in the right place, they were all fully functioning and actively involved with torches, pitchers and trumpets. There was no chance for inactivity!

Ephesians 4 tells us that we shall come to fullness of stature when every part is working properly. Gideon's army would have been destroyed if some had been missing. Imagine the chaos if one shouted, and then another, while others grouped together to shine their lights. We must all be in our places and working properly; then the impact will be enormous.

The great contrast between Gideon's army and the church today is that each member had identical tasks, whereas the church displays infinite variety. God has blessed us with such a variety of gifts which, added together, make the church wonderful and glorious. Consider for a moment the diversity and spectacular beauty of the creation. Wildlife programmes on television often give us privileged glimpses of multi-coloured flora and fauna, of forests, mountains, lakes and seas. We see infinite variety. God has not even made two snowflakes alike and yet, incredibly, all creation is going to be wrapped up as a garment and thrown away. But his church will live for ever. His glorious church with all its variety is the pinnacle of God's creative skill. Is it right that we should go to church on Sundays merely to sing four hymns, hear a sermon and then go home? What a waste of all God's wonderful gifts. Remember, only the church survives—the rest of creation will be cast away. The seas, mountains and forests have not captivated him—however much they impress us—but the beautiful, wonderful, multi-coloured church God will keep for ever.

I remember an elderly man in a church that I used to visit occasionally. One day I asked him how he was and for a quarter of an hour he poured out his sorrows. On my next visit I forgot my previous experience and recklessly asked him again! He repeated his tale of woe. Amazingly, it happened a third time. On this occasion I felt I must speak, reminding him that for the believer life was anything but negative. Months later I visited the church again and noticed my friend looking very different. He told me that God had given him a little ministry. It transpired that he had been obtaining old birthday cards, inserting fresh inside pages and, in beautiful copperplate handwriting, had filled them with scriptures and poems. These he had sent out to the lonely and the elderly—to anybody he heard was in need. He then showed me letters of gratitude he had received from many who had been helped by his unusual but delightful ministry.

When Paul lists his gifts of the Holy Spirit I do not remember one entitled 'writing poems in old birthday cards', but there are such a variety of ways in which we can encourage one another that not one of us needs to remain unfulfilled. That man's life was transformed as he found a lovely ministry appropriate for him at his stage in life. God wants every one of us in the right place, working fully and effectively in his glorious church.

## Cast on God

Finally, Gideon's army was not only characterized by its unity and its use of spiritual weapons, but also by tactics that were totally dependent on God. They did not adopt the attitude that they had to do everything themselves nor did they passively say, 'It's all God's work—we are "letting go and letting God." We just hand it all over to him and he will do it.' The battle of Midian reveals a beautiful balance of human responsibility and divine intervention. We must not be passively waiting for angelic activity. We must seek God for strategy. Amazingly, we are co-workers with God! We fellowship with him in the work. Although God could triumph without us, he invites us to be involved in his plan. He has different strategies for different battles. The strategy for taking Jericho was to walk round it and shout. The strategy for Ai was to set up an ambush. So we must not assume that because a certain method worked on one occasion, from now on that is the accepted pattern! God will not be shut into a formula or method. He wants to share his plans with us so that we get to know him.

Gideon's army was united. Each member was in the right place at the right time, and functioning properly. They had a strategy, but they were totally dependent on God. In this context, he was able to move. The Midianites did not flee merely because of some noise and a few moments of confusion. They fled because God set the sword of each one against another throughout the army. Gideon's manoeuvres, no matter how skilfully accomplished, could not destroy an army. God stepped in!

We must continually seek God for his strategy in our generation and then ask for his powerful presence to transform our endeavours into God-like proportions

Gideon's victory was total. The Midianites were devastated and fled. With great rejoicing they pursued their enemies and totally routed them in memorable triumph.

## A last word

Before closing, we must see one final lesson from this battle. Gideon now invited all the men of Ephraim to become involved in the rout of Midian. There was no attempt to claim victory exclusively for his hand-picked 300. He wanted the whole nation involved. When some men of Ephraim challenged him with exclusiveness, he was quick to disarm them with his open-heartedness. He drew them in. It was not in his heart to lead a small, separate, elitist group. He had seen God move with power and there had been a great victory, but Gideon wanted to share it with *all* the Lord's people.

Today there is no room for any to claim special status in the conflict. God is for all his people, so we must learn to be like him and welcome one another in the love of Christ.

We began by noting that Isaiah 9 promises the ever-increasing government of Christ and likens its advance to the battle of Midian. But to thoroughly rout Midian and see Christ's kingdom triumph we must all unite and take the battlefield together. Past misunderstandings, divisions and hurts must be put away. If God's kingdom is to be established, forgiveness must prevail. Forgetting what is behind, we must press on, reaching forward to what lies ahead. May God enable us to learn the lessons and fulfil God's purpose in our generation thus proving ourselves to be truly men and women of destiny.

# NEHEMIAH

'The God of heaven will give us success; therefore we His servants will arise and build' (Neh 2:20).

# 14

# *Blessed Are Those Who Mourn*

There came a day in the life of Nehemiah which started like any other but, by the end of that day, he was a changed man. The motivation for his life, and his expectations concerning his career were transformed.

God could do that for you as you read this book. He could come to you and turn your life upside-down. You may have thought, 'I have my career, I know my path in life,' but God can come to you and speak to you in such a way as to make your career insignificant. Like Nehemiah, you could discover. 'From now on Zion is my chief delight. From now on to see the city rebuilt, to seethe church of God restored from ruins is the pre-eminent factor in my life.' It could happen in one day. It can happen listening to one sermon.

One day Moses was with the same sheep on the same routine, when suddenly he saw a bush burning! His life was never the same again! That day started like any other day, but a burning bush made all the difference.

One day David was looking after a few of his father's sheep, when one of his brothers came rushing up the hill panting out the message, 'David, Samuel is here. He wants to see you!' David hurried off to his memorable encounter with Samuel. His life was never the same again!

One day Isaiah was in the house of God. Israel's great king had died and Isaiah faced the future with concern, when suddenly he saw the Lord high and lifted up. In a moment his life was revolutionized.

Gideon, frightened little Gideon, was hiding away. Suddenly, an angel of the Lord spoke to him. That was his turning point.

Paul, breathing out threats and slaughter against the church, suddenly saw a light!

One day God-fearing Nehemiah in his safe, secure job simply heard some news. But it changed his life completely. The whole course of his life was transformed that day. What news did he hear? 'The wall of Jerusalem is broken down, and its gates are burned with fire.' Years earlier, pioneers had returned from captivity in Babylon to rebuild Jerusalem from its ruins. The city of God had been desecrated, but Nehemiah thought the rebuilding was well under way by now. Instead, Zion was a pathetic heap of rubbish. The walls were down. Anybody could walk in. The gates were burned. They were 'in great distress, shame and reproach'. Nehemiah was overwhelmed with the news.' He was devastated.

### Take heed how you hear

As I reflected on this, it occurred to me that we can be very bad hearers of news. Jesus said, 'Take heed how you hear.' Today we have so much information coming at us from television, radio and newspapers, that devastating news can be heard so passively, so indifferently; we can be so preoccupied.

We can, for instance, see news about a drought in Africa and be deeply moved for a moment, seeing tiny children with their emaciated bodies. The news is starkly real and our hearts go out to them. But then there is the next item of news, followed by another and, as is so often the case, the news comes to a conclusion with something

utterly trivial: 'And finally today it was reported that....'
It is inserted as a nightly dose of aspirin to help us through
the traumas and tragedies that constitute the real news.
Often at the end of a news programme we see something
comic or mildly absurd—perhaps a dog has learned to ride
a bicycle—and we smile to ourselves and go on to the next
programme, forgetting the terrible plight of people in
Ethiopia or an earthquake in Mexico City.

We hear news all the time but we do not know *how* to
hear it. 'Take heed *how* you hear.' We can be moved for a
moment and yet not have heard enough to change us. But
Nehemiah heard and that was all it took. He was devastated. Oh that we might be so sensitive!

You may be driving along a motorway listening to
music on the radio. You hear one tune after another, and
you may even hear an appeal for 'The Week's Good
Cause' and be moved for a moment. That is one way of
listening. But there is another way of listening. Suddenly
the announcer interrupts the programme with: 'Here is a
call for Mr and Mrs Robinson travelling in Lancashire.
Their son is in hospital in London, seriously ill.' If you are
those Robinsons, you hear *that* news differently! You are
gripped. You stop. You change direction.

That is how we need to hear. Jesus said, 'The heart of
this people has become dull, and with their ears they
scarcely hear (Mt 13:15). Listen to these words of Jesus:

> Then He will also say to those on His left, 'Depart from Me,
> accursed ones, into the eternal fire which has been prepared
> for the devil and his angels...these will go away into eternal
> punishment, but the righteous into eternal life (Mt 25:41–46).

How well did you hear? Isn't it true that we have
become dull of hearing. We find it very difficult to hear
'these will go away into eternal punishment'.

Jesus said, 'Take heed how you hear. This people's
hearts have become dull, their ears barely hear.' But God

says from heaven, 'This is my beloved Son—*hear him*. He understands about life and death. He understands about eternity. He dwelt in eternity with me. He knows and can speak with authority about eternal matters. Beloved, *hear him*. He is my dear Son.' Have we heard the news? Has it gripped us? Has it devastated us?

## A glorious church

Hear another piece of news. Jesus wants a spotless, perfect Bride, 'fair as the moon, clear as the sun, and terrible as an army with banners' (Song 6:10, AV). That is what he wants. That is what he is going to have. When we consider how glorious Zion is meant to be, are we overwhelmed by the thought and the vision? It can only happen when we realize that God has declared that Christ died for a glorious church.

We need to be overwhelmed before we can become useful to God. We need to look at the situation of the church today, and we need to look at our society where the walls which say, 'This is acceptable and this is not acceptable,' are down. In the very beginning God separated light and darkness, and ever since then he has been in the business of separating and dividing. So it is a great tragedy when the walls of society crumble.

Without any doubt the walls are coming down. Our society is afflicted with the scourge of AIDS and other diseases that owe their origin to promiscuity. Yet the cry is not, 'How can we stop promiscuity?' but rather, 'How can we cure AIDS?' It could be argued that in society there have never been clear distinctives. But the real tragedy is when the walls come down in church life. The newspapers recently reported a Methodist minister who gave his blessing to a lesbian marriage. Where was the wall that said, 'No, that is not acceptable inside the church of God'?

Let me show you what the world thinks of the church.

Recently a national newspaper carried an article by a political journalist—not a religious columnist, but a political expert who writes regularly for that newspaper. Under the heading 'You Can't Sell Faith Like Cornflakes' he said this about the church:

Over the past generation, a process of demoralisation has set in among the clergy. Watching their flocks diminish, they have tended to hold less strongly to their own convictions or, rather, they have found secular substitutes for a dogmatic religious faith which is waning. In place of the Christianity of the ten commandments they have put their Christianity of social welfare. They concern themselves with what they imagine are burning topical issues. They hold debates on nuclear weapons, some of them campaign actively on behalf of pacifist bodies, preach sermons on unemployment. Sometimes they behave as though they were little more than social workers. Sometimes they try to usurp the functions of government ministers. They are almost invariably well-meaning, progressive-minded, humanitarian and, to use the current catchphrase, caring and compassionate. But there is nothing more to distinguish these high-minded bishops, deans, canons and reverends from any other category of do-gooders. The charismatic element seems to have gone. They are manifestly not divinely inspired. There is not much faith in their hearts or fire in their bellies, and it shows! It seems to me that there is absolutely no future for the church as a social welfare institution. At the same time, the church has watered down its teaching on almost all aspects of morality. If young people seek guidance on sexual conduct, for instance, they are no longer offered definite rules but are given polysyllabic fudge and mush. People turn to God not in order to seek their own materialist, earthly desires, but to escape from them.

The church is meant to offer something which is better and ennobling. Religion is not about this world—it is about the next. Christianity is not a secular crusade for social improvements—it is an alternative to materialism. A rejection of the world and the flesh, it concentrates instead on the eternal and the divine. The notion that it can be democratised and popularised is nonsense. It operates on the frontiers of human understanding and makes heroic demands of its adherents. That indeed is precisely its appeal: because it is so totally and constitutionally different from anything else to be found in the world. Of course, to preach this kind of Christianity—the only true kind—requires a passionate faith which is very uncharacteristic of many churchmen. Preferring to operate with the techniques of modern religious sociology they are in fact getting absolutely nowhere.

The journalist's article did not conclude with biblical answers, but he was able to discern the shambles. He was saying, 'Look, they are being compassionate and caring like any other do-gooders, but where is their distinctive message? Are they not supposed to be distinctive and different?' He concluded that the whole thing is humbug. The photograph over the article was a communion service being celebrated on Centre Court, Wimbledon! The world says 'Nonsense! We are not impressed!'

The world regards the church as irrelevant to modern living. We need to hear that news. The walls are down and the world can see it! The gates are not there—anybody can walk in and say anything. And that is where the story begins—when people, young men and women, older people, like Nehemiah, hear this news in such a way that it triggers something off within them and they cry, 'Enough! We cannot stand this any longer.' God has said that his city will be the joy of the whole earth and the world says that it is humbug! This realization must come to us with such force that we cannot stand still any longer. The shame should hit us hard.

Nehemiah felt that igniting spark trigger something deep within his spirit. Has it happened to you yet? Has Zion become the chief motivation in your life? You may be a school teacher or a nurse or an insurance salesman, but can you truly say that the kingdom of God comes first? Everything else has to take second place. For some of us this is going to mean that we can no longer be a teacher, a nurse, or a salesman. We will find that we must give our lives to rebuilding the city of God.

## Weeping first, working later

First of all, Nehemiah heard the news. Secondly, he cried to God. In his need Nehemiah wept, mourned, fasted and prayed. His first response was not action. If our first response is action we betray the fact that we have failed to see the enormity of the problem. We simply have not understood. The situation has not overwhelmed us. We have not sat down and wept. To think we can just put on a crusade and change things is like administering aspirin to someone with terminal cancer. It is a hopeless endeavour. We have to fall down, mourn and pray.

Some of us are at ease because we have the biggest church in town. But what is 2–300 people in a town of 30,000? What is 1,000 in an urban area of 300,000? Our churches may have become the largest in town, but what is that against the vast crowds who do not know that Jesus is alive and think that the church is a joke? We must allow that to hurt us. It must penetrate us to the core. When Nehemiah considered the reality it overwhelmed him!

Until we have wept over the ruins, we will never build the wall. If we have begun to see scores of people crowding into our churches and been tempted to think that we have hit the jackpot, we should go from door to door where 5,000 people live on a local housing estate and ask them how interested they are in Jesus. When the reality overwhelms us we shall start crying to God. The Bible does not say, 'Have a go.' It does not say, 'Blessed are the whiz-kids who know how to get the publicity moving,' or, 'Blessed are those who know how to use the media.' Instead it says, 'Blessed are those who mourn.' Why? Because they shall be *fortified*. 'Fortified' is a better translation than 'comforted'. When the Bible was first translated into English, 'comfort' carried the meaning that 'fortify' has retained today. When we think about comfort, we think about cushions and armchairs, but when the Bible says, 'Blessed are those who mourn, for they shall be comforted,' and, 'I will send the Comforter,' it means something more than ease and rest.

Our basic understanding of the Holy Spirit's ministry has been affected by the way this English word has changed its meaning. When Wycliffe first penned the word it meant 'to fortify, strengthen, provoke or stir up'. Today it carries more of a 'there, there' meaning. Our hymnbooks often reflect this with their gentle hymns about the Holy Spirit: 'There, there, don't worry—the Holy Spirit will comfort.' No! The word is 'fortify'!

I believe that Nehemiah grieved red-eyed in the dust, crying out, 'Lord, this is so disgraceful, so shameful, that your city should come to this!' Such a heartfelt response is an alien concept to many who call themselves evangelical. But so often we are coldly evangelical, divisively evangelical, traditionally evangelical, withstanding-the-Holy-Ghost evangelical! We stand on our traditions and claim we are true to the Bible, but still say 'No' to the Holy Spirit. In repentance we must admit, 'Oh God, it is shameful that your house is in ruins.'

When we humbly begin to agree with God, he can begin to fortify us: 'Blessed are those who mourn, for they shall be fortified.'

Nehemiah was first of all overwhelmed by the reality. It consumed him. His chief thought was, 'The city of God is in ruins.' We too, must be gripped by the enormity of the problem so that God can begin to fortify us. Nehemiah turned to God as his only answer. God is our only answer too—not simply trying special meetings, not endeavouring to manipulate the media. We need God! It is as basic as that! After his mourning, Nehemiah was transformed, fortified, commissioned! From that time on, no obstacle thrown across his path could stop him!

# 15

## *Passion for Zion*

When Nehemiah began to pray, his prayer was one of the most memorable and instructive prayers in the Bible. First of all he cried out to the *God of heaven*. When we see our own puny endeavours we can be so grateful that our God is the God of the heavens, the eternal God, the glorious God. Great and marvellous, he rides on the heavens to our help. It is when we see the enormity of our problems that we are absolutely cast on him—not to bless our puny ideas but to take over. The God of the heavens is our only hope. We need heaven's power, heaven's resources and heaven's conviction. We need God to move in convicting power to bring about revival. I was deeply stirred when I read about J. O. Fraser's experiences in China as recorded in *Mountain Rain*. He made prayer his major occupation and, after several years, hundreds of families in many villages were swept into the kingdom.

### The great and terrible God

When Nehemiah cried out to 'the God of the heavens', he addressed him as 'the great and terrible God'. Nehemiah was not fooled into thinking that God had diminished in power because the nation was in need and the city was in

ruins. He still believed that he was the great and terrible
God. We need to rediscover the majesty of our God. He is
great and terrible—so much bigger than our subjective
view of him. That is why it is so edifying to sing great
truths about God that come straight from the pages of
Scripture rather than derive our doctrine of God from
sentimental songs and hymns.

When we read of Zechariah, for instance, we probably
think of him as a prophet of encouragement—and he
certainly was—but the very first word that Zechariah
prophesied was the word 'angry'. Zechariah 1 reads, 'The
Lord was very angry with your fathers.' It was because
God was angry that he sent his people into humiliating
captivity in Babylon. We have such a plastic view of God
that we tend to forget that he can be angry. When they
returned to Jerusalem as a 'restoration people' they still
failed to build and Zechariah had to say to them, 'Listen,
God was angry with your fathers. Do not think, just
because you have come back and have experienced some
of God's blessing, that you can drift along. No! God has
not changed. He still requires wholehearted commitment
to his purposes.' He is still the great and terrible God. It is
a fearful thing to fall into the hands of the living God and
we must never forget it.

Moving from that foundation, Nehemiah began to
reckon on another great truth. He addressed God as the
One 'who keeps his covenant of love with those who love
him and keep his commandments'. Although he is angry,
although he is great and terrible, he is also the God of
covenant love with his people. He has made a covenant
with his chosen. He has determined a future for them. Let
us take note as we see how Nehemiah pressed on in
intercession: 'Father, I know you are great, I know you
are awesome, I know you are terrible, but, Lord, we are
your people and you have made a covenant.' If we are to
be effective intercessors it is vital to be persuaded that we
come to a God of covenant love. We can pray, 'Lord, you

made a covenant with us in your dear Son. We may be weak at present, but you are for us, you are with us!'

We can begin to argue our case. Prayer is arguing your case. Look at the greatest pray-ers of the Bible—they are arguing the case: 'Lord, if this is so, what about this?' Abraham is a good example. He argues, 'Lord, if there are this many righteous, will you save the city? Lord, if there are *this* many... ?' Look at Moses. He said, 'God, if I have found favour, if I have found grace, show me your glory'—arguing from one thing to the next. Do you argue your case before God? We need to pray, 'Lord you have promised,' so that we plead the promises as our way to receive mighty answers. He is a covenant-keeping God with whom we may dare to argue.

Nehemiah said, 'Remember the word which Thou didst command Thy servant Moses (Neh 1:8). That is the way to pray: 'Lord, *you* said it. It is not *our* idea.' That is why Elijah prayed that the rain would stop. It was not just Elijah's bright idea. He did not think, 'What shall I pray to impress the people? I know, I will pray that the rain will stop.' He did not suddenly have a brainwave. He knew that Deuteronomy said 'If you go after false gods, I will shut the heavens, I will stop the rain' (see Deuteronomy 11:17). He knew what God had promised and how to argue those promises with God.

Nehemiah was not going to experiment with his own schemes. He was cast on God: 'God, you promised. I am pleading the case before you now!' Moving on, we see that Nehemiah also identified with the sin of the nation. He said, '*We* have sinned!' We need to identify. We need to say, 'O God, we are part of this church that is a laughing stock.' We would like to stand back from it and not be associated with something that is seen as a weak, irrelevant anachronism, but we are part of the whole. As we acknowledge our common identity as children of God, we will feel the weight of responsibility and become strongly-motivated intercessors.

Next, Nehemiah reminded God, 'Lord, your word says that if we turn against you, you will scatter us; but if we turn to you, you will gather us again to the place that you have chosen to cause your name to dwell.' It is interesting to note that in God's purpose scattering represents judgement and gathering is part of blessing. God is gathering a people in these days. Have you been gathered, as it says here, 'to a place where he is causing his name to dwell'? Gathering is a part of God's mercy in renewal so that he can manifest his name and glory.

Then Nehemiah used this last argument. He said, 'They are *your* people.' I underlined in my Bible all the places where it says 'your' in Nehemiah 1:10. 'They are *your* servants and *your* people whom *you* redeemed by *your* great strength and *your* mighty hand' (NIV). Nehemiah threw the whole onus back onto God. He said, 'Lord, these are your people. There is an awful mess, but they are yours, Lord.'

Moses used the same method when he argued, 'Lord, they are your people. What will the heathen say? That you are not able to bring them into the land?' Jesus did the same thing in John 17: 'Yours they were and you gave them to me. Now, Lord, I am committing them to you. They are yours, Lord. Your name is attached to them.' We must bring that argument to God when we say, 'O God, we are your beloved people, your church, your great name is involved!' Do you prevail with God like that? God is looking for people who will. We are so casual. God is looking for people who will come before him and plead for his church and his great name—'Blessed are those who mourn, for they shall be fortified!'

## Nehemiah commissioned

This opening chapter shows Nehemiah a broken-hearted man, but after his encounter with God he never looked back. He started by weeping, fasting and crying, but after this chapter it did not matter what problems he encountered—absolutely nothing was going to stop him. Talk about a fortified man! He was marvellous! He leaps out from the pages—a wonderful three-dimensional figure! Why? Because God fortified him. God strengthened him. God came to him in his mourning.

Do you mourn your poverty-stricken spirit? You are really blessed. Why? Because you refuse to depend on your own resources. If you are poor in spirit you are in a position to receive grace, so don't despair, say instead, 'Thank you, Lord. The situation is overwhelming but you can fortify me.'

## Ex-cupbearer

At the very end of the first chapter, Nehemiah added one important detail: 'Now I was the cupbearer to the king.' This highly significant role as cupbearer to the king no longer held any real importance—he didn't use this privileged rank to impress his readers, he merely mentioned it at the end. His priorities were established.

We do not know about God's secret dealings with Nehemiah. What we would term 'Nehemiah's call' is not recorded for us, but during those days with God, those days of prayer, clearly God began to deal with him. After his encounter with God he could say to the king, 'Send me to Judah, to the city of my fathers' tombs.' That phrase 'the city of my fathers' tombs' really caught my attention. He had a sense of history. He wanted to go back to the city where his fathers were. He was gripped by the honour of his family.

You might well argue that that does not apply to you. You are the only one in your family who is converted to Christ. You do not come from a Christian background. No, you are thinking about the wrong family. Once you are born again you belong to another family altogether. Zion is the city of your family and your fathers' tombs.

There are amazing tombs in Zion—did you know that?
Tombs of great men and women down through the ages.
You have joined a wonderful family. Wesley was in it.
Whitefield was in it.

I have recently been reading about some of the great
reformers; men who laid down their lives like Tyndale
who translated the Scriptures. Such men are our fathers.
Their tombs are there. Reading again, after many years,
J. C. Ryle's book *Five Great Reformers* I met once more
Bishop Hooper as he laid down his life in the flames. A
reformer to the end, he prevailed for the truth, even
though it meant being condemned to the stake. Three
times they had to light the firewood around his legs. The
first time it just blazed up, burned his arm and went out!
After they had lit the flames again the wind changed
direction, but this man stood bound to the stake saying
wonderful, glorious things about his Saviour.

These heroes are part of our family! They have gone
before us in order to give us the Scriptures, in order to see
the church of God come to fullness. We need to say, 'Let
me see the city of my fathers' tombs again.'

'I want to see a city that is worthy of their sacrifice.'

'I want to see a church that speaks of the glory of these
men who laid down their lives.'


## I will rebuild it

Nehemiah said, 'Send me to Judah, to the city of my
fathers' tombs that I may rebuild it.' He was so stirred by
the challenge that he said, 'I am going to rebuild it'—
almost implying that even if no one else went, he was still
going to build it! How foreign to the thinking which says,
'*Someone* ought to do *something* about it. We will draw up
a committee.' The men who got things done never
thought like that. Let the whole scheme be totally impossible, they would still say, 'I am going to build it!' These are
the men and women who change situations, who find,

once they start building, that there is a whole army to help them. They do not say, '*Someone* ought to do something,' they themselves seek God until he ignites a fire in their hearts and then cry, 'Let me get to it; let me see your church restored!'

Don't you long for the day when in every town, in every place, there is a glorious testimony—hundreds of worshipping, praising people?

Every year we hold a youth conference at a holiday camp on the south coast. As we praise and worship God in the ballroom every evening, the staff are always amazed to see so many young people excited about God. They have commented, 'It's a pity the church isn't like this!' How true that is! The world has no time for empty religion; it has no time for our arguing about whether the chairs should be facing this way or that, or whether we should raise our hands in meetings. They are bewildered that the church majors on such trivialities. They don't mind us taking over their holiday camp and making a lot of noise. They are used to people making noise. Christians have this strange preoccupation with little things: 'We have always done it this way.'

We claim to have the answer to the world's needs. Many of us claim to be scrupulously evangelical and are horrified at hearing the news of lesbian marriages being blessed in other churches. But still we are preoccupied with the importance of chairs facing the right way! Meanwhile, the world regards us as irrelevant, and who can blame them?

When the world sees reality they will be open-mouthed. They will say, 'We didn't know the church was like this!' They will throng to see it. Amazed by it, they will look forward to us coming. If we are obedient we shall see more and more blessing. It will be tough, as we shall see through chapter after chapter of Nehemiah's experience. A hornets' nest will be stirred up when we, like Nehemiah, have the welfare of God's people as our first love rather than the status quo.

We have to be possessed with the same passion as our fathers before us. It is hopeless to settle for the status quo saying, 'We have our traditions here.' They had their traditions when they burned Hooper at the stake and when Tyndale was hounded to his death. That is why they killed them. Where is the spirit of the reformers? Where are the people who will say, 'Persecute me if you will, but I am going to rebuild the house of God!' We have got to have that brand of passion. It may be impossible, but Nehemiah boldly affirmed, 'I am going to rebuild. I am going to do something about it!'

# 16

## *It Was Very Displeasing to Them*

How suddenly Nehemiah's whole life was changed! His established routine was transformed by what he heard and he became a man of destiny.

A young pastor from Switzerland attended one of our conferences for ministers. He had been developing his church in a fairly traditional way and then, suddenly, one day he heard about God's purpose to restore the church. 'Now I am ruined,' he said. 'I cannot settle for anything less.'

Nehemiah became a man gripped by a vision. His burden was to see Zion restored, her walls standing, her gates strong and firm and the purposes of God established. But fulfilling that vision involved a battle. Powerful enemies opposed him. 'When Sanballat...and Tobiah... heard about it, it was very displeasing to them that some-one had come to seek the welfare of the sons of Israel' (Neh 2:10).

As you read on, you find that this displeasure quickly developed into fury and anger (Neh 4:1). We have a spiritual enemy, the devil, who is furious that the church is being restored. He was so happy to see it in disarray and lacking in faith and a sense of destiny. To see the church beginning to gain fresh impetus; to see Christians arise like Nehemiah, purposing to rebuild, brings trembling and fear, anger and fury into the enemy camp. He therefore provokes conflict. It has not been easy to restore the church. Bruised and battered, we have come through many crises as the spiritual battle rages.

As we consider the story of Nehemiah, we shall find the devil trying many different schemes to prevent the rebuilding of the city. We shall also discover many amazing parallels with our contemporary scene. The devil tries many disguises. If one trick does not work, he switches to another in his hostility to the church. Remember, he is not just interested in little you! He wants to stop the whole city being built and, in as much as you are part of that, he attacks you. Every way he can he will try to stop the rebuilding programme. Throughout the conflict it is vital that we remember that our battle is not against flesh and blood, but against spiritual forces opposed to God.

## Mighty mockery!

The first weapon he chose to use was mockery. They began to laugh.

> It came about that when Sanballat heard that we were rebuilding the wall, he became furious and very angry and mocked the Jews. And he spoke in the presence of his brothers and the wealthy men of Samaria and said, 'What are these feeble Jews doing? Are they going to restore it for themselves? Can they offer sacrifices? Can they finish in a day? Can they revive the stones from the dusty rubble, even the burned ones?' Now Tobiah the Ammonite was near him and he said, 'Even what they are building—if a fox should jump on it, he would break their stone wall down!' (Neh 4:1–3).

Taken at face value, mockery sounds as though it is an expression of indifference, but the Bible reveals what was behind it all. They were not indifferent at all. They were furious and angry and were using mockery as a deliberate weapon.

The devil is very cunning. He knows our flesh. He knows how we hate to be ridiculed. Man naturally wants to be honoured and respected. He wants to be accepted, not laughed at, and many will desert from the spiritual battlefield because of the pain inflicted through mockery. If secret pride hides in our hearts, mockery will certainly bring it to the surface and uncover our hidden motivations.

Sanballat was not alone either. He poured scorn on the Jews 'before his brothers and the *wealthy men of Samaria*'. Ridicule from the sophisticated 'in crowd' is hard to bear. Those who seem to have 'got it together' can use the weapon with devastating force.

Often Christian women with unconverted husbands have to endure mockery such as: 'Surely you're not going to that silly church again with all those gullible people,' aimed at unsettling their new-found faith. Sometimes teenagers experience similar comments from unconverted parents: 'Don't you realize that modern science has disproved Christianity.' It sounds so casual but can be so powerful and inflict deep wounds. If we are going to triumph over this enemy of ours we must face up to the fact that the gospel is foolishness to the natural man. We are tempted to pray for successful sportsmen and pop singers, or the most popular figure in our university to be saved so that we can have some of our pride back. We often think, 'If only a prestigious person could be saved, we could all stand up and say, 'He is a scientist and he's a Christian.'

No, the gospel is folly! The natural man thinks it is nonsense that our hopes are built on Jesus of Nazareth who died on a cross in the Middle East 2,000 years ago. It is nonsense to modern twentieth-century man. But we must also remember that it was nonsense to the Greeks of Paul's day and that he endured mockery in Athens. Experiencing sarcasm and scorn is part of taking up our cross and following our beloved Lord Jesus, who endured mockery to the end.

Ridicule is not only used to attack the faith of individuals. In Nehemiah's day it was used to oppose the restoration programme. They said, 'Even if a fox ran up there, the whole thing would collapse!' You can imagine their critics laughing at them. Often, twentieth-century attempts at the restoration of the church have been similarly attacked. 'They call themselves a church, but they don't even have a proper clergy or a proper church building! There is no scholarship among them! What serious theologian is allied with them? It will all blow over in a few years.'

## Crippling compromise

Because ridicule and scorn did not stop Nehemiah, his opponents resorted to another approach. They had confidently predicted that nothing would prosper but 'the walls got to half their height and the people had a mind to work'. Jerusalem was beginning to take on some stature and a look of permanence. The whole project was taking off—with growth and progress all around. So they turned to their next weapon, namely, compromise. 'Let us meet together, let us talk about this. Hold on a minute, you're moving at quite a pace—it looks as though it's going to stand after all. We need to have a round table conference.' The context shows that their plan was actually to destroy the work of God, but it came in the guise of 'having a talk about things'. The ugly weapon of compromise!

I look back to when I was a young Christian, longing to be filled with the Holy Spirit. I remember spending a whole evening in my bedroom praying about receiving the Holy Spirit. I was longing to find the answer. At the end of the evening, my door opened and my father most lovingly said to me, 'Come on, son, you mustn't take this religion so seriously.' Have you heard that sort of thing? Have you

heard, 'Don't take it too seriously. We don't mind you
going to church on Sunday, but you must keep things in
proportion. That church of yours is not like other
churches—they get very noisy down there! Why do you
take it all so seriously?'

Many face this challenge especially after God has called
them into full-time service or to some other particular
step of commitment. We hear such reasonable arguments
as, 'Be careful. You cannot refuse that promotion—
you've been waiting for it for years and you deserve it.
Think what it will mean for your income.' If the devil
cannot laugh us out of court he whispers, 'For goodness'
sake, don't take it so seriously.'

The cajoling is so persuasive: 'You cannot give up all
that. The promotion would give you a very influential
position. In your spare time you could still do a lot for the
church. Be reasonable!' The call to sweet reason can be a
powerful weapon in the enemy's hand: 'God wants you to
be reasonable. He doesn't want you to be fanatical.' So
doubt is sown in our minds: 'Am I being fanatical? Perhaps
I am being short-sighted. Am I throwing everything
away?' The battle rages as the devil tries to destroy the
onward purpose of your life and the advance of the restoration of the church.

I am sure you have met people who ask, 'Why must you
insist on speaking in tongues and all that noisy worship?
Why don't you do that elsewhere and leave us to have our
Sunday services as we have always had them? Why don't
you show love and keep others happy? If you must have
that charismatic meeting, you can have it in your own
house, but let's keep Sunday decent and in order. A lot of
people in the church don't like it. Remember, the Holy
Spirit never brings division—the Holy Spirit is always
loving.' This kind of reasoning can have crippling power,
especially when a recently baptized-in-the-Spirit young
preacher has his salary, his home, his wife and children
and his whole security to think of. He realizes that to be

true to his vision might well result in a loss of all material security. Rightly he thinks, 'Where shall we live? What shall we do? I suppose I could compromise. Perhaps we could have just a few Scripture songs and perhaps I could ask people not to raise their hands on a Sunday, and we could somehow settle at a level where everybody is happy.'

A pastor recently told me that he had resigned from his local church. He acknowledged, 'For too long I tried leading from the middle, and you cannot do it.' He had been trying to keep everybody happy, but in the end the situation nearly destroyed him.

Nehemiah refused to compromise. He was gripped by a vision to see Zion restored and the walls erected. The apostle Paul was driven by a similar commitment. He saw himself as one called by God and entrusted with the gospel, and therefore made it his aim to speak 'not as pleasing men but God, who examines our hearts' (1 Thess 2:4). Paul knew that his final examination would be before the throne of God and he was more concerned to please his God than simply to please man. And though at all times he tried to put no stumbling block in the way of others, nothing would prevent his obedience to the vision that God had put before him.

If we are to fulfil our calling and the purpose of God in our generation, we shall have to learn to overcome the challenge of mockery and compromise—but the battle does not end here. Satan had more weapons in his arsenal, as we shall go on to see.

# 17

# 'It Is Reported—You Are to Be Their King'

Nehemiah's enemies had not finished yet. They tried a third powerful weapon. Sanballat sent his servant to Nehemiah with an open letter in which was written: 'It is reported among the nations, and Gashmu says, that you and the Jews are planning to rebel; therefore you are rebuilding the wall. And you are to be their king, according to these reports' (Neh 6:6). Here was the next attack. First mockery, then compromise, and now—flagrant lies! 'It is reported...' and 'we have someone here who says it's true...'. What was reported? 'You are starting a rebellion, a takeover—and you are to be the king. And you have also appointed prophets to proclaim concerning you, "A king is in Judah!".' In other words, Nehemiah was being attacked for setting up an authority structure.

How incredible! This could have been written in the 1980s. Such misrepresentation is common today: 'We know your game! You're forming a new power structure, and you're going to be the new Pope!' With a quick addition of 'There's no smoke without fire,' accusations fly left, right and centre.

I was recently invited by a group of ministers to explain the theology of our church. I happily responded to the invitation, but pointed out to them that we were not

inventing a new theology but were simply, as evangelicals, trying to be whole-heartedly biblical. I spoke
briefly and then suggested that they might like to ask
questions. The rest of our time together was spent in
answering those questions. Towards the end, they asked
about our 'authority structure' within the church. They
explained, 'We have heard that if anybody in your church
wants to redecorate their home or buy new furniture, they
have to get permission.' Turning to one of their members,
they indicated that he had told them that this was the case.
Immediately, the man denied that he had first-hand
knowledge but had simply heard it from somebody else.
Each one in turn denied that they had been the original
one to report this rumour.

Happily, I was able to put their minds at rest, and say
that we were not in the slightest bit interested in directing
people concerning their house decorations or furniture.

Amazingly, they then produced another even more
incredible story. This time they prefaced their remarks by
assuring me that they knew that this particular case was
true because one of their number had been acquainted
with the facts. It seems that they had heard that a couple
wanted to join our church. The wife was acceptable to us
but the husband was not, so we had required them to be
divorced before she could join. I sat there appalled! I
asked which of the men present could give me more
details of the case, since I knew nothing at all about it.
Incredibly, the same thing that had happened before was
repeated, namely, not one of the men acknowledged that
they actually knew anything about it personally. We
paused while different ones around the circle said, 'Surely,
*you* told us about it, didn't you?' All denied being the
original source of this story too. My heart was very heavy
as I pleaded with them, 'Brethren, neither of these things
is true and none of you seem to know where the original
stories came from.'

Tragically, in our constituency we are having to learn to

live with these rumours all the time. When we have reported them back to our congregations, from time to time, I think it would be true to say that our people usually howl with laughter, though in all honesty I think we do not know whether to laugh or cry.

Nehemiah's opponents challenged his motivation. They claimed that he wanted to be king. What a total and tragic fabrication and distortion of facts. Nothing could have been further from the truth! The Bible tells us what Nehemiah's motivation was—he was broken-hearted about the condition of Jerusalem, he longed to see Zion restored. That was his only motivation. He wanted to see Zion changed into a city set on a hill which could not be hid. He wanted to replace piles of rubbish with clear-cut walls and gates. He wanted to see the purpose of God fulfilled in his generation.

### Formidable fear

Fear was their next device. Shemaiah said to Nehemiah, 'Let us meet together in the house of God, within the temple, and let us close the doors of the temple, for they are coming to kill you, and they are coming to kill you at night' (Neh 6:10). Nehemiah was encouraged to withdraw to a place of safety. The subtlety was that Shemaiah appeared to be a friend.

'Your life is in danger, Nehemiah. Run into the house of God and find safety!' Fear is a formidable weapon, especially when a friend comes, pleading caution: 'What will happen to you if you stay on this course?' Jesus knew this experience as he was heading to Jerusalem. A friend of his said, 'Not the cross, Lord.' Jesus retorted, 'Get behind me, Satan.' Peter longed for Jesus to save his life, and others will introduce fear into our hearts as they make similar pleas like: 'If you go this way, it will cost you your home, your job—everything.' Nevertheless, we have a Saviour who said that the way to find our lives was to lose them, thereby delivering us from fear. When we yield to fear we rob ourselves of the wonder of proving God's faithfulness in the midst of difficulty.

## Destructive disloyalty

Now we turn to perhaps the ugliest of all strategems used by the devil.

> In those days many letters went from the nobles of Judah to Tobiah, and Tobiah's letters came to them. For many in Judah were bound by oath to him...Moreover, they were speaking about his good deeds in my presence and reported my words to him (Neh 6:17–19).

Disloyalty is a wicked, cruel weapon. Many who apparently supported Nehemiah were actually bound by oath to Tobiah, his enemy. One of the greatest agonies that a servant of God has to endure takes place when one who apparently supports you turns to become disloyal. All other enemies are external, but disloyalty penetrates and wounds the heart.

Once again, our Lord Jesus was tempted in all things like we are and his experience is referred to prophetically in Psalm 55:

> His speech was smoother than butter, but his heart was war; his words were softer than oil, yet they were drawn swords... for it is not an enemy who reproaches me, then I could bear it; nor is it one who hates me who has exalted himself against me; then I could hide myself from him. But it is you, a man my equal, my companion and my familiar friend. We who had sweet fellowship together, walked in the house of God in the throng. (vv. 21, 12).

Jesus knew what it was to be betrayed by a kiss.

God hates disloyalty. He delights in covenant love and wants us to be a loyal people. May I ask you, are you loyal or do you have feet in two camps? Do you apparently support one church, but really give your allegiance somewhere else? In Nehemiah's day key people were involved, such as some of the nobles. Tragically, today we can find some in leadership—perhaps men who are deacons—promising allegiance to their paster, but who still go to others complaining: 'We really do not like the way in which this man is taking our church. I'm going to retain my office of deacon so as to withstand him and hold the church on course.'

Alternatively, it might be that you belong to a church that does not want to embrace spiritual renewal and restoration. You remain there, though you have no heart for it nor faith that it will ever change. In fact, you enjoy more fellowship with a mid-week charismatic group than you do with the church you attend on Sundays. You attend that church, but express no true loyalty to it. I would like to suggest that we cannot have a foot in each camp. Either way, we will hurt our brothers by being double minded. If churches choose to close their doors to charismatic worship, they must be prepared to recognize the fact that they are also closing their doors to charismatic worshippers, who must be free to go and find fellowship where they will. It is hardly fair to then describe them as divisive.

God wants us to be a loyal people. He wants us to be whole-heartedly committed to a local church. We must be real and make up our minds and give consistent loyalty to a church and leadership that we can whole-heartedly support.

Actually, where there is true Christian grace, this can be accomplished without pain and backlash. Men can honestly and humbly agree to differ and go their separate ways, and thankfully this has often happened. Tragically, however, there has often been pain, and usually it would be true to say that neither party could claim to be free from sin in the way things were handled.

Though Nehemiah was confronted by powerful obstacles to his progress, he overcame them all. We have noted that he was initially fortified to cope with the task before him. Now we must turn to see how he particularly withstood Satan in the various disguises that we have mentioned.

# 18

## *So We Built the Wall*

How did Nehemiah overcome this barrage of attacks? In
his determination to rebuild the walls, he brushed aside
every assault that Satan hurled at him.

He overcame mockery very simply by just getting on
with the job. They laughed at Nehemiah. They said,
'They cannot build on all this rubbish. If a fox ran up, it
would fall over.' Nehemiah gave the best possible
answer—he built the wall. When people mock you, your
best response is simply to 'build the wall'—be true to your
convictions. You do not need to retaliate or try to vindicate yourself. Simply build up the walls of God in your
life. You Christian ladies with non-Christian husbands, or
young people who have been saved at university and then
come home to your parents who complain that they didn't
send you to university to become a religious fanatic—do
not argue! Just build the walls. Let your life shine. Let
people observe that the wall is being built—your character
is developing. Be respectful, sensitive, righteous and
clean. Do not become easily offended.

Inwardly Nehemiah said, 'Hear, O Lord! [*You* listen,
because *I* haven't time! I'm building the wall!]' He did not
get taken up with the mockery. He did not allow himself
to be affected by it. Having mourned, he was now forti-

fied. They could mock as much as they liked—he just built the wall.

Finally, the fact that the wall stood was proof that God was with him. The same must be true for the current work of restoration in the church. We do not have to vindicate ourselves. By all means let us graciously answer when we are asked questions, but let us keep building, let us stay on course, keep going, keep working and let the fruit speak for itself.

Then he overcame the compromise by replying: 'I am doing a great work and I cannot come down. Why should the work stop while I leave it and come down to you?' (Neh 6:3). There is so much discussion today. So many groups and committees want to have yet another meeting of evangelical leaders to discuss all that is happening. We have to be very selective or else we shall be for ever on committees discussing what might happen next!

Nehemiah said, 'I am doing a great work. I cannot come down. I cannot be for ever debating the implication of what I am doing. I have to obey God and fulfil his purpose.' He was not going to be hoodwinked into merely talking about it.

Perhaps the phrase 'I am doing a great work. I cannot come down' reminds you of another man. His opponents said to him, 'If you are some great one, why don't you come down?' From the cross he could have answered similarly, 'I am doing a great work. I will not come down.' Dear friends, we have to identify with that cross. It can be very flattering to be invited to committees to discuss the implications of our work for the church today, but we need to allow God to help us to know when to go and when to say, 'I'm sorry, but I'm about a great work. I cannot come down. I cannot for ever be discussing whether I should make my work more palatable to the church at large.'

Then followed the mischievous lies. Amazingly, Nehemiah seemed comparatively untroubled by them.

He dismissed them: 'Such things as you are saying have not been done, but you are inventing them in your own mind' (Neh 6:8). That was the end of it. We must emulate him. We cannot be taken up with chasing these mysterious allegations or trying to unravel where they all start. Just as Nehemiah did not seem to become preoccupied with it or thrown off course, neither must we be. We must press on!

Next came fear. Nehemiah's answer was clear: 'Should a man like me flee? And could one such as I go into the temple to save his life? I will not go in' (Neh 6:11). What a mighty answer! Arrogant? No, he was not arrogant. He had a sense of destiny. He had no intention of running away or being diverted.

Then followed the fifth line of attack—disloyalty. The story provides no answer to disloyalty. Nehemiah's heart was broken. Those of you whose hearts have been broken through the disloyalty of those whom you thought you could trust know the agony. You know what it feels like. There is no answer. You have to learn to bear it and make sure that the seed of bitterness is not sown in your spirit. If someone lets you down, beware the root of bitterness that grows up and spoils not only you but everyone who comes near you. It may hurt, but you must not allow your spirit to be soured.

I notice that Nehemiah learned the lesson very quickly. In the very next chapter (Neh 7:2) we find that when the wall was rebuilt and the doors set in place the gatekeepers and the singers and the Levites were appointed: 'I put Hanani my brother, and Hananiah the commander of the fortress, in charge of Jerusalem, for he was a faithful man and feared God more than many.' When we are wounded by the disloyal we must make sure that next time we build on loyal people. That is what Nehemiah did. He did not react, he simply made sure that the next man he built on was loyal and feared the Lord. Those to whom God will entrust responsibility may not appear to be as significant as the nobles who were disloyal. They may not be public figures, but they must be loyal men of integrity who fear God.

## Such a man as I

What made Nehemiah so steadfast? What kept him going through such opposition? First, his call: 'Such a man as I.' He was not arrogant or full of self-importance, but he was aware that God had apprehended him. In his time of deep sorrow concerning the situation in Jerusalem, God met with him and fortified him by the Holy Spirit. He knew he had been chosen.

We can be fortified by similar truth. He has chosen us before the world was formed to be holy and blameless before him. He has predestined us. We become strong when we realize that God, out of his great wisdom and knowledge, has reached down to us through eternal ages. He has chosen us. We may be weak and feeble, but he has chosen to use us. For this reason we can say, 'I am not going to flee. Should such a man as I flee? God has chosen me!'

In Philippians 3 the apostle Paul introduces us to the most wonderful 'that' in the Bible: 'I press on in order that I may lay hold of *that* for which I was laid hold of by Christ Jesus' (Phil 3:12). Paul is saying here, 'Eternal God laid hold of me. I was a rebel; I was an opponent of the gospel, and Christ laid hold of me.'

If you are a Christian that is true of you too. Your conversion may not have been very dramatic; you may not have seen a light blazing around you, but if you are a Christian the verse is nevertheless true of you. Christ laid hold of you. It does not matter if you say, 'But I simply came from a Christian home.' There are plenty of people who have come from Christian homes who have not followed on to know the Lord, but for every one of us who does know the Lord, the truth is that Christ laid hold of us. There is a 'that' which is tied up with your life and mine—'*that* for which he laid hold of you'.

Paul said that he was pressing after this. His consuming passion was to lay hold of *that* for which God laid hold of him. That was the all-consuming passion of his life. Paul had a destiny and a dignity. He was not just being tossed about by the circumstances of life. And neither are you nor I in this world of cynicism and indifference, where people ask despairingly, 'Who can really change anything?' People feel so hopeless, even in our democratic system. What can we do? Knowing that God has laid hold of us makes all the difference. God has laid hold of us for a purpose—to give us a destiny. We must reply, 'I am going to lay hold of that for which you laid hold of me.' Nehemiah was aware that he was a called person.

When Nehemiah responded so zealously he found a whole company of people responding with him. His passion was to rebuild Jerusalem, and when he arrived on the scene he discovered a whole army of people who said, 'Let us arise and build.' They had a corporate sense of destiny. Today, many have a corporate sense of destiny. We are gripped with the awareness that our Bible Weeks are not merely annual conventions, nor just a few sessions of Bible teaching providing escapism from the awful world. Destiny grips us. God is doing a great work and we feel involved.

For decades the church has been in the doldrums, but now God is rebuilding it and we are part of that activity of his Spirit. Thousands are being affected. In his mercy, God is using us. How can we be taken up with lesser things? The King of Glory is going to make his church shine again and he has involved us in his great plan. We are helping to prepare the way.

Not that we are anything special. Nehemiah was nothing, but by virtue of his call and his awareness of that call he said, 'Should such a man as I flee? I am in the will of God.' May I ask, does the will of God grip and thrill you? Nehemiah could not escape God's call on his life, but embraced it with total commitment and used it as a weapon to overcome every enemy. He was armed with purpose—not aimless and therefore vulnerable.

## Total commitment

Secondly, the call was matched by commitment. Nehemiah 4:23 reports: 'None of us removed our clothes, each took his weapon even to the water.' The sword and the trowel! We are going to build the church in the same way. We are going to raise this house in the midst of our enemies who do not want us to. With sword and trowel we shall fight and build. Some people built during the day and were on guard-duty all night. They were totally committed to the work. Why? Because they were convinced that it was a great project. Are you committed to the great project of glorifying Jesus in the earth and saving poor sinners? Or do you think that the church is simply a nice place to attend? I rejoice to see more and more people taking up the challenge of whole-hearted commitment to Christ and his church.

## Remember the Lord

Thirdly, Nehemiah reassured the people, 'Do not be afraid of them; remember the Lord who is great and awesome, and fight' (Neh 4:14). What a mighty statement that is. We need a revelation of our great and terrible God and then we need to fight, assured of his sufficiency. Be strong in the Lord and in the power of his might. If you are not strong in the Lord, the devil will penetrate with his fiery darts. Be strong because you *must be*, and be strong because you *can be*! Remember the Lord, who is great and terrible, and fight. The God of heaven will give us success if we have absolute confidence in him.

## Comradeship

Fourthly, Nehemiah grouped men together. In panic some were terrified of being overrun: 'They will come up against us from every place' (Neh 4:12). So Nehemiah 'stationed men behind the lowest parts of the space behind the wall, the exposed places, and stationed the people in families with their swords, spears, and bows'. What comradeship as they all stood together! Sometimes they were separated from one another because of the length of the wall, so Nehemiah instructed them to sound the trumpet in the event of an attack: 'At whatever place you hear the sound of the trumpet, rally to us there' (Neh 4:20). This comradeship should characterize our church life. We should not go through pressures alone any more. Of course, our personal relationship with the Lord is vital to our spiritual life, but we also need to blow the trumpet so that people can rush to help and take the load.

I remember when my wife was about five months pregnant with one of our children, and I was away at a conference. Suddenly the membrane containing the water surrounding the embryo was punctured. My wife immediately took to her bed and telephoned some ladies from the church who promptly rushed in, took our children and looked after everything. Later the doctor said that the child might easily have been lost had it not been that she lay down so quickly. Because of our dear friends, our baby survived! My wife blew the trumpet and the people rushed to help. Is your church like that? Or does nobody even know that you belong? God wants his church to be a community where, if you pick up the phone, there are people ready to lend a hand. They rush in and they care! The church may be growing larger and larger, but there has to be a company who know you and care for you.

Also, if we are in distress we need to be increasingly open; not self-sufficient and independent, but willing to ask for help. Don't sweat things out on your own, too proud to be honest, so that when you are asked, 'How are things?' you conceal your real need under a superficial, 'Fine, thank you.' God wants us to be more honest than that. When you are under pressure, blow the trumpet. Cry out for help.

I remember a men's meeting many years ago when a policeman friend of mine arrived utterly exhausted. He arrived rather late in a crowded room of men and said, 'I am shattered.' I must confess that at the time I thought, 'What a great way to start a meeting!' But as he began to share about what he had been through that day, which included the sort of heartaches that police in our modern society have to endure, the presence of God began to be manifested in that room. There was a beautiful sharing of the load and I still remember that evening as one of our most remarkable times of spiritual breakthrough. Here was a brother blowing the trumpet. He did not conceal his need superficially, but shared his pain. God owned the reality and we were able to worship him in Spirit and truth.

Sometimes pressure comes to your part of the wall. If you do not shout, we will not necessarily know about it. We must build a sense of comradeship into our relationships.

### 'Hear me, O God'

Nehemiah's final weapon is clearly seen as that of constant prayer. When you read through the book of Nehemiah you cannot fail to see the many verses where Nehemiah cries, 'Hear me, O God!' From the outset he was a man of prayer. Chapter 1 records his long intercessory prayer, but then in chapter 2 we eavesdrop on his meeting with the king: 'What do you request?' the king asks. A beautiful autobiographical detail follows: 'So I said to the Lord and I answered the king.' That was how Nehemiah lived all the time.

Later, he had no time even to change his clothes from one day to the next, but he was constantly crying out, 'God, hear what my enemy is saying!' Unceasingly he prayed, 'Hear, O God!'

All the time he was asking God to strengthen his hands. Just like Jesus, his prayers were ceaseless. We will never see what God has for us without developing a similar lifestyle of constant prayer to God. That was how Nehemiah overcame and that was how Jesus prevailed. The early disciples learned the lesson from Jesus and devoted themselves to prayer. Prayer undergirded all their activity—never was it dull or routine, but always in the context of gospel advance. On the day of Pentecost they prayed and fire fell. A few days later they prayed and the house shook and they were freshly filled with the Holy Spirit and boldness. News of Peter's imprisonment inspired them not to storm the jail but to storm the heavens in earnest intercession which led to his release. We must similarly bathe all our activities in believing prayer if we are to enjoy the kind of success that Nehemiah experienced.

So Nehemiah brushed aside every attack launched against him. With steadfast determination he pressed towards his goal. He knew that God had apprehended him and, like Jesus, his food was to do the will of him who sent him and to finish his work (Jn 4:34). Nothing could deflect him from his course. May God inspire in us a similar devotion and determination, so that in our day the church may be restored to beauty and strength and be a Bride worthy of her wonderful Lord.

# 19

## Becoming a Community

Having won the battle, what next? Nehemiah also had to form the people into a loving community. When the external battle fades from view we often begin to find problems within. When we are no longer cast against a common enemy we begin to have difficulties with one another. When the enemy is outside we all unsheath our swords and work together as an army in the frontline, but when the enemy is no longer attacking we notice details overlooked before—'You didn't lay that brick very well! You just dropped your trowel on my foot!'

We must begin with a fervent determination to be one people. Nehemiah 8:1 tells us that 'all the people gathered as one man'. This refrain appears again in verse 12—'All the people went away to eat, to drink.' It does not say that some of them said, 'No, the situation is too serious. We must stay here.' The command came, 'Do not be grieved, for the joy of the Lord is your strength.' So they all went. They had all come to listen to Ezra and now they all departed to do as they had been told. When they discovered in the law that they should celebrate the Feast of Tabernacles 'the entire assembly did it'. The Scriptures do not say, 'Some zealous ones obeyed, but others thought that it wasn't a good idea.' No, the entire assembly complied. A mighty unity of purpose took hold of them. We must be similarly motivated if we are to see the church restored.

## A 'nobody' or a 'somebody'?

What are some of the enemies of unity? In 1 Corinthians 12 Paul unexpectedly pointed out that the first to break the unity are those who disqualify themselves. He tells us that the foot cannot say, 'Because I am not a hand, I am not a part of the body' (verse 15). Some of us say, 'I am only a foot. No one notices me.' What we mean is, 'I am no problem to unity really, since I am just a nobody.' Actually, we bring disunity when we adopt that attitude because a 'dead' member is disunited from the living body, thereby frustrating the grace of God in the whole. So Paul says, 'Beware of saying you are a nobody.'

When we embrace that attitude we begin to take a back seat. Gradually, we drift into becoming mere spectators. Uninvolved in the battle, we sit on the terraces and can often find we are being tempted to criticize, since we can easily observe other people's errors. Paul's counsel is that we should be united by finding our place in the body and therefore be thoroughly fulfilled!

In the same chapter Paul swings to address the self-important who also bring disunity. Some people are so full of themselves that they do not need others. In conversation they simply wait for you to finish so that they can have their say. Whenever you share your news with them they have information to trump yours! Those who argue 'I have no need of you' display the self-importance that frustrates unity in the body.

## Loving encounters

The fearful who will not confront also bring disunity. When someone is continually offending us we must ask

God for courage to act. When we do not confront we leave a vulnerable area for the devil, who tempts us to indulge in criticism and gossip. When a third party is critical of the one you feel is in error, you are easily drawn in. So one of the ways we overcome disunity is to find the love and courage to confront others. The Bible says, 'Admonish one another,' and, 'Exhort one another every day.' If we are going to become a true community or family, we have to find grace to speak into one another's lives and overcome the fear of being rejected. Elders in a local church must certainly be able to check one another. If leaders paper over their differences, the flock will soon become aware of the cracks.

## Free forgiveness

Those who refuse to forgive also prevent true unity. This is so obvious that I do not need to spend a lot of time on it, except to say this: Christians may have many faults, but they should excel at forgiving! We should all be magnificent forgivers even if we fail in other areas. We may not be able to sing, or serve, or organize very well, but we should be brilliant at forgiving because we have all been forgiven. If we are not first-class at forgiving then it is questionable whether we really know the grace of God. We ought to be gold medallists at it!

Another person who breaks the unity is the legalist—the one who lives by his rules and condemns those who do not. He fragments the body. He lives by a very rigid rule-book and, having been diligent to do that himself, is greatly offended by the freedom of others. Romans 14 warns us against such a stance. We are not to pass judgement on other people's liberty, nor are we to despise other people's consciences. We must allow each man to stand before his God and answer for himself.

A further cause of disunity in a local church is the 'watchdog' who is there ensuring that the pastor 'does not take things too far'. He feels he is to safeguard the church from error and excess! Such a man brings disunity. He feels he is serving God, but he is spoiling the progress of that local church.

In longing for unity we must be willing to lose our individualism. I do not say lose our identity—God treasures the uniqueness of the individual, but he deplores our independence. Are you one who always demands that everything must be explained to you? Do you insist that you must always be satisfied when leaders invite you to join them in a certain course? Are you responsive, or do you reply, 'I will do so if God tells me to'? Some are continually defensive, aloof and unwilling wholly to cast in their lot with God's people. If you are such a person, you are frustrating the unity which God seeks. By all means discuss your difficulties, but do not be defensive. Be willing to lose your life in order that you might find it.

## Value people for themselves

Sometimes our very zeal for God can condemn others who begin to feel they are not valued as people but only in terms of what they can accomplish. They do not feel beloved and precious. God wants us genuinely to rejoice in one another. If we continually pressurize one another to be doing more, the whole church becomes riddled with striving and self-effort. God wants a unity based on grace that is all-embracing, loving and accepting, without a whiff of condemnation.

Will you be determined then to be of one heart? It is the priority of the New Testament. Peter says, '*Above all*, keep fervent in your love for one another' (1 Pet 4:8). Do not merely put up with one another, but be fervent in love.

Some argue that the trouble with our sort of church is that we all think the same, but that is exactly what Paul expected! He exhorts us to be 'made complete in the same mind and in the same judgment' (1 Cor 1:10). Clearly, Paul does not mean that we have to become so submissive that we are not allowed to think for ourselves. We can arrive at whole-hearted agreement with joy and faith. The New Testament norm is that we are perfectly joined together in one mind and one judgement. For the sake of unity we must refuse to indulge in the luxury of being offended, disapproving, critical and intolerant.

For Nehemiah, 'all the people gathered as one man'. To maintain this unity will require all our energies, but this is what the Lord Jesus expects of us. Paul pleaded with the Ephesians to make every effort to maintain the unity of the Spirit in the bond of peace (Eph 4:3). In that great chapter are included some of the most glorious descriptions of the church in the whole Bible. He saw the body of Christ being built up until we all reach unity in the faith and in the knowledge of the Son of God, and becoming mature, attaining to the whole measure of the fullness of Christ (Eph 4:12–13).

In order to reach that magnificent climax, however, we must be completely humble and gentle; be patient, bearing with one another in love (Eph 4:2). We must speak the truth in love and, finally, build ourselves up in love as each part does its work (Eph 4:15–16).

All this requires sustained determination to receive one another as Christ received us and to retain humble attitudes of love and acceptance at all times. Only then will the house of God be restored in glory in the earth, and Jesus receive the praise of which he is worthy.

# 20

# *Building on Truth*

The next key factor in forming these returned exiles into a community was supplied by Ezra the teacher who 'brought the law before the assembly of men, women, and all who could listen with understanding' (Neh 8:2). It was crucial that their recovery programme and expression of loving unity was based on the revealed word of God. Ezra was a vital restoration figure!

In seeking a recovery of New Testament church life, we are not merely arguing for the reinstatement of speaking in tongues and prophesying. We want to see the Bible restored to its rightful place as the final authority for church life. Ezra was not dismissed as 'merely a Bible teacher'. On the contrary, they built him a podium in the centre of the square and 'all the people gathered as one man' to hear hear him. His teaching brought a genuine touch of revival which they had not previously known.

Some people in the early days of the charismatic movement were so hostile to the perils of the one-man ministry that they turned against prepared teaching in favour of a spontaneous form of 'body ministry'. They tried to live on a diet of spontaneous sharing and regarded prepared Bible exposition as 'old hat'. This was, of course, a tragic mistake.

I recall attending a church where, after a lively time of praise, one brother stood and exhorted everybody to be real. He then gave a five-minute talk on openness and transparency. After more praise, a second brother rose to his feet and to my amazement called us to be *really* real! No other preaching took place. The church cannot expect to grow on a diet of exhortations to be 'really real'! Some expressed their frustration with their former experience of cold Bible teaching by arguing that the early Christians had no Bible. It was argued that throughout the first centuries of the church Christians did not carry a big black Bible with them, therefore we also should simply 'be yourself in the Spirit'! Some charismatics have clearly given the impression that they are anti-Bible.

If, however, we see the book of Nehemiah as a guide-book to restoration we could never take that path as we see the central role that Ezra fulfilled. Most of the churches to which I am related have about an hour's Bible teaching on a typical Sunday morning.

We must always remember that Jesus came as a teacher sent from God. He went everywhere teaching the kingdom. Even after he had been raised from the dead he continued to teach. If ever there was a time when teaching would seem unnecessary it was then, but he did not just turn up and say, 'Look, I'm back!' Instead he opened the Scriptures and, starting with Moses and all the prophets, he spoke to them of all the things concerning himself. It was not enough simply to appear. The apostles were not persecuted by their opponents for filling Jerusalem with their miracles, but for filling Jerusalem with their *teaching*.

Although it could be argued that first-century Christians had no black Bibles, it is clearly recorded that they devoted themselves to the apostles' doctrine and that Paul claimed to have taught them day and night, clearly instructing Timothy to guard the form of sound doctrine and to pass it on to others who are able, in turn, to communicate it faithfully. On one occasion we read of the

apostle Paul preaching all night, interrupted only by a
swift resurrection job on a boy who fell from the window!
Paul would hardly have been content to give the impression that all the young Christians needed to do was 'to live
from their spirit'.

## Truth to safeguard us

The word of God must take central place to safeguard us
from errors, both old and new. We are warned that in the
last days there will come doctrines of demons; there will
come strange new ideas that people with itching ears will
follow. Many are already abroad today. We need to be
clearly grounded in the Scriptures so that we are not
vulnerable to counterfeit signs and wonders.

Similarly, we must beware of old strange doctrines
which explain away the Bible and give greater place to
tradition than they do to the revealed truth. Jesus said to
the men of his day, 'You have a fine way of disregarding
the word of God so that you might keep your own traditions' (see Matthew 15:6). We need to bring every tradition in our church life to this book and ask, 'Is it in the
book? If it is not in the Bible, why do we do it?'

The word of God will inspire a true knowledge of God.
To know him is eternal life. We need to know objective
truth. We rejoice in that intuitive knowledge that comes
from the Spirit and reveals Christ to us, but the Bible tells
us wonderful things about God which we would not know
intuitively. We would not know what the cross meant
unless the Bible explained it to us. Other events in Jesus'
life and throughout the Bible are only understood as we
seek God's own interpretation of those events as recorded
in Scripture.

If we bow to the authority of Scripture instead of bowing
to almighty tradition, we would see what church worship
is meant to be like. We would see the place of apostles and
prophets if we would only ask, 'What does the book say?'

Does it suggest that the ministries listed in Ephesians 4 should cease by the end of the first century? Does the Bible actually say that there were only twelve apostles? It does not! We must bow to the authority of Scripture in our restoration recovery and reformation. The Reformation of Luther's day provided a glorious dawn, but left many shadows in church life. For a full recovery of New Testament church life, we must yield ourselves to the word of God as they did in Ezra's day.

### The truth sets us free

Knowing the truth releases us. We need to know what happened to us when Jesus died. Gospel truth not only prepares us for heaven—it releases us for life in the present. We need to know that our old self was crucified with him and that he who has died is free from sin (Rom 6:6–7). Many are condemned because they do not know. Many are still living under the oppression of the law because they do not know that Christ is the end of the law to everyone who believes. Many live under a heavy cloud because they do not know that there is no condemnation for those who are in Christ Jesus.

Through the very great and precious promises, God has given us everything we need for life and godliness (2 Pet 1:3–4). The victory that overcomes the world is our faith, and faith comes through hearing the word of God. The word of God, then, is central to restoration both in our individual lives and in our church life.

I remember being in a cathedral in Barcelona a few years ago. I had gone to visit my sister who was a missionary there and I had a little time before catching the plane home. I was sitting in the cathedral looking around, when in came a frail old lady dressed in black, her back bent double. She bought a candle, lit it and placed it in front of a statue. Putting a veil over her head, she sat there looking up at the statue—and I thought of the words of Jesus.

There must have been many things that lady needed. She was poor, she was bent over, but the thing she needed more than anything else was this—that someone teach her many things. 'Seeing the crowd like sheep without a shepherd, Jesus had compassion on them and taught them many things.'

# 21

## *What a Celebration!*

Next to be restored was the celebration of the Feast of Tabernacles, or the Feast of Booths. So they went into the hill country and cut down branches from the trees to make booths, or tents, and for a whole week they lived in them. But why? They were remembering their true identity. They were saying, 'Although we are building this city we are actually a pilgrim people.' Though they were building something solid and substantial, they had to remember as true children of God that earthly Jerusalem was not their final destination. Abraham, their pilgrim father, with the eye of faith had seen a city with foundations, whose maker and builder was God. From that day on, Abraham no longer lived in Ur of the Chaldees but made his home in a tent. Every time they celebrated the Feast of Tabernacles they were remembering the same truth.

The same must be true for us. Although we want to build something substantial in our generation, our eyes must still be focused on the glorious hope that will be revealed to us at the coming of our Lord Jesus. We have the blessed hope of a magnificent future! We must constantly remember that we are a people whose roots are somewhere else and that we are here only temporarily. The very essence of a tent is impermanence; put up in an hour, blown down in five minutes!

Paul tells us, '[Christ] gave Himself for our sins, that He might deliver us out of this present evil age' (Gal 1:4). We are not only delivered from sin, guilt and punishment, but delivered out of this present age. Again we are told, 'Let those of us who have dealings with this world be as though we had no dealings with it.' We must have dealings with the world, but we are no longer to be dominated by it. 'Living in tents' is to be our lifestyle. We must not let the world squeeze us into its mould. The night is almost gone and day is at hand! We are children of the day, not of the night, so do not get taken up with something that is going to vanish in a moment of time. The book of Revelation tells us that great Babylon, that mighty city, will crumble to dust in one hour. We live in a passing age—don't get caught up in it!

The international, worldwide outpouring of the Holy Spirit is heralding and preparing the way for the return of Christ. It is almost here. Why give our lives to lesser things? Let us remember where our hope lies. Paul said, 'We exult in hope of the glory of God' (Rom 5:2). Our ultimate hope must not be focused only on the restoration of the church but on the coming of Jesus. We may prophesy, but we only prophesy in part. There may be tongues, but they will cease. When the perfect comes, the partial disappears. Now we see in a mirror dimly, but then face to face.

Not long ago I listened to a tape by A. W. Tozer. I had never heard this twentieth-century prophet on tape before. His writings are challenging enough! His address was on Isaiah 6 and I wondered if I was ready to hear Tozer on Isaiah 6. Apprehensively I switched on the tape. He began, 'Tonight I am going to speak about the holiness of God. I am a fool. No one should speak about it for we know nothing about it.' That spiritual giant of a man declared himself a fool to speak of what he knew nothing about! Dear friends, we know a little pin-prick of truth and it has transformed us. What will it be like when we see him? In moments of worship we catch glimpses of his glory, but what will it be to see him face to face?

God may have given you a lovely home or a healthy body but, remember, really it is only a tent: 'For we know that if the earthly tent which is our house is torn down, we have a building from God, a house not made with hands, eternal in the heavens' (2 Cor 5:1). God may have blessed us with material provision, but let us make sure that our eyes are fixed on the unseen and the eternal.

As the Israelites dwelt in tents for their Feast of Tabernacles they were remembering their true identity as the people of God. We too shall be seen as different to society round about us, not simply by building successful churches but by having a totally different approach to life because we have no fear of death and are looking forward to meeting Jesus.

### Rediscover your roots

In the ninth chapter of Nehemiah we read that the next thing the Israelites did was to recount their history. We need to know our roots. To hear charismatics pray sometimes, you would think that the church only started five years ago! Many of us have no grasp of what God has been doing through the ages. Often our prayer and praise times reflect this short-sighted view. It is pointless for us to live in the past, but let us be clear—the church has not just arrived on the scene. We have a wonderful heritage! If we want to know our identity we must rediscover our roots and be aware of church history.

When I was first saved I lived on a diet of biographies! I thank God for men like Hudson Taylor, Murray McCheyne, George Muller, Praying Hyde, George Whitefield, to name a few. We have a wonderful family tree! Do you know about them? Let me encourage you to read the lives of such men and rub shoulders with these giants. They are our forefathers and we need to rediscover the histories of these amazing men and women. You will feel very much at home with many of them. Read Ian Murray and rediscover the 'Puritan hope'. Their hope coincides very much with yours. Read *The Pilgrim Church* by Broadbent and you will find that you are part of a great ongoing move of God. Study it. Be stimulated and strengthened by it.

As the pioneering settlers were restored in Jerusalem, they must have derived great comfort as they rehearsed their history together as recorded in Nehemiah 9. They were able to catch the grand sweep of God's purposes and see something of the overall plan of God, thereby underlining their own sense of identity.

### Triumphant worship

With a growing sense of purpose they completed the building of the walls and arranged a celebratory dedication—a festival of praise! They brought the Levites to Jerusalem so that they might celebrate the dedication with hymns of thanksgiving and the music of cymbals, harps and lyres. Nehemiah arranged for the leaders of Judah to mount the wall and appointed two great choirs to march around it.

Tobiah had said that if even a fox had climbed up these walls, they would have fallen down, but now choirs were marching on them. What a day of celebration!

When they concluded their triumphant march they offered great sacrifices and rejoiced. Even the women and children rejoiced so that the joy of Jerusalem was heard from afar. How fitting it was that they should celebrate in this way. And how much more fitting it is for the church of God to display joy unspeakable and full of glory. Triumphant praise will be one of the marks of the church in the last days. It should have been so throughout the ages!

When Paul was looking for that distinctive sign of a true church, which would mark it out from others, he said in Philippians 3:3 'We are the true circumcision, who worship in the Spirit of God.' He could have used so many different phrases to describe the true church. He could have said 'We are the true circumcision who believe in the atonement,' which would have been very true. He could have argued, 'We are the true circumcision who have direct access to the early apostles.' But instead he said, 'We are the true circumcision, who worship in the Spirit of God and glory in Christ Jesus and put no confidence in the flesh.'

So if you arrive in a town wondering where the true church of God is in that location, a biblical way of identifying them according to Paul's letter is that the true people of God will be those who are worshipping in the Spirit. This will mark them out—it will be one of the identifiable things about them. Paul could have said that the true circumcision were those who were true in doctrine, but actually if you find a company who are *truly* worshipping in the Spirit, you have found a church which has already spent time in sorting out many other things. They have won many victories. And if they are worshipping in Spirit and in truth, love and unity must be prevailing.

Worshipping by the Spirit does not come easily to a local church. It does not happen overnight. The book of Nehemiah does not start with marching, rejoicing choirs and orchestras on the top of the walls, but it does arrive there eventually!

I rejoice to see the growing orchestras in local churches today. It is very thrilling to see the diversity of instruments and to see young people contributing to worship. I have seen trumpets and trombones, saxophones and clarinets, harps and oboes, violins and cellos, not to mention modern synthesizers and electric guitars.

I well remember the first Sunday when loud clashing cymbals were played at my home church in Brighton. As we sang one of the great hymns, I saw a light suddenly flash and wondered what it was. No, it wasn't a heavenly visitation! Light was being reflected on two great cymbals that were being taken out of a shopping bag. We were singing one of those magnificent old hymns, like 'Praise the Lord, His glories show'. The 'hallelujah' which concludes each line was now accompanied by the enthusiastic crash of those shining cymbals. It was wonderful! There are some instruments that speak of the majesty of God and while the old harmonium is not one of them—the clashing cymbal most certainly is! God is worthy of all our enthusiasm and the combination of all our skills.

A revolution has been taking place! Englishmen, as respectable as any invented, who formerly kept their hands battened resolutely at their hips as though they did not trust them out alone, have suddenly become hand-clapping, hand-raising enthusiasts!

Joyful praise and heartfelt worship have in many churches replaced the formal hymn-singing which used to provide merely the prelude to the all-important preaching. 'Participation' has become a key word superceding passivity. Growing numbers of people are taking part in congregational worship with spoken and sung prophecies, tongues and interpretation, shared visions, or in playing musical instruments among growing church orchestras.

The manifestation of the presence of God has, on occasions, become almost breathtaking in its intensity, evoking sometimes shouts of joy and other times tears of devoted adoration.

Prophetic songs have multiplied, focusing our vision on the city of God, the government of Christ and the purpose of God to reach the nations through a glorious church. Beautiful worship songs have melted our hearts and helped us to recognize the Lord's personal and intimate love for us. We have stood or knelt in his presence with great delight. Hymn-boards and bored hymn-singers have largely become relics of the past!

It has become so edifying to sing passages of Scripture set to music so that we are meditating on truth as well as worshipping the Lord. The Lord is seeking those who will worship him in Spirit and truth, and I believe he is finding them in increasing numbers.

Over the last decade the burgeoning Bible Weeks have created settings for jubilant praise. A growing army of whole-hearted believers, accompanied by orchestras with trumpets and crashing cymbals, feel that 'the shout of the King is among them'! 'All hail King Jesus' has become not only an expression of love but also a declaration of war as we freshly commit ourselves to our King and his kingdom and, as his Bride, make ourselves ready for his return with heartfelt joy.

Gradually God is filling out our worship. It is becoming more worthy of him. Restored worship is one of the most significant features that characterize our church life. 'The joy of Jerusalem was heard from afar' (Neh 12:43).

# 22

# *Throw Him Out!*

As a preacher I was greatly tempted to forget that after the triumphant choirs of Nehemiah 12 come the disappointments of Nehemiah 13. How lovely it would be to conclude the Bible Week at the end of chapter 12 while the choirs were still singing! Chapter 13 seems such an embarrassing anti-climax! In my preparation I prayed, 'Please, Father, may I finish on chapter 12?' and I felt quite clearly God say to me, 'No, you may not. Not only may you not finish on that note of glory and praise, but you must look at chapter 13 and faithfully teach on it on the last night.' In the final analysis, life simply does not consist of Bible Weeks or Feasts of Tabernacles.

God instigated three great festivals in the Jewish national year when they would gather to him without distraction. But God knows, and we know, that the real crunch comes not while we are with thousands of others· singing praises, but when we return to our normal real-life situation. Nehemiah 13 uncompromisingly reminds us of that truth. We should not test Bible Weeks by how exciting it was to be there. A more realistic test would be to ask ourselves how much our lives have changed. Thank God for the numerous people who have testified that their lives have been dramatically and lastingly changed at previous

Bible Weeks. Whole churches have been transformed as a result of coming together in numbers and corporately embracing God's prophetic purpose and entering into new dimensions of love, fellowship and praise. Nevertheless, we know that when we return to our normal lifestyle many challenges await us.

Chapter 13 recounts how Nehemiah returned to Babylon. Then, after a period of time (how long is not absolutely clear), he came back to Jerusalem and discovered to his horror that the people of God had very sadly backslidden from the euphoria of those earlier days. They had failed to retain their pioneering clarity.

## A little leaven

In Nehemiah's absence 'Eliashib the priest...being related to Tobiah, had prepared a large room for him where formerly they put...the utensils, and the tithes of grain, wine and oil prescribed for the Levites' (Neh 13: 4–5). On his return, however, Nehemiah recorded:

> I came to Jerusalem and learned about the evil that Eliashib had done for Tobiah, by preparing a room for him in the courts of the house of God. And it was very displeasing to me, so I threw all of Tobiah's household goods out of the room. Then I gave an order and they cleansed the rooms; and I returned there the utensils of the house of God with the grain offerings and the frankincense (13:7–9).

Nehemiah returned to find Tobiah housed in a room within the very house of God. Tobiah was the one who, at the beginning, had said, 'Even if a fox ran up, the whole thing would fall down!' He had also sent letters to frighten Nehemiah and some had been disloyally bound by oath to him. He had been a constant thorn in the flesh for Nehemiah and now here he was, right back in centre of the life of Zion in the house of God!

Now what is the New Testament significance for us in this picture? As I was before God I felt that he reminded me of a clear parallel—an enemy of the gospel, first of all mocking, then opposing and, finally, trying to join in the very life of the church. It seems to me that the apostle Paul had to fight his own 'Tobiah' who appeared on the scene in the form of *legalism*.

Let me explain what I mean. At first, the legalists, personified by the Pharisees, heard and withstood John the Baptist as he prepared the way for the Lord. Like Tobiah, they claimed to be the true people of the land. They were Abraham's sons! When Jesus arrived on the scene they withstood him. They mocked him as the son of a carpenter; they noticed that no serious Pharisee was following him. Later, as Jesus' following was gathering momentum, their mockery changed to serious debate. They tried to catch him in his words; they brought clever arguments asking, 'Should we pay taxes to Caesar or not?' They tried to force him into debate. They told lies and brought many false accusations.

Later, as the early church triumphed, with multitudes being converted, many priests became obedient to the faith. Later still, thousands of the Jews believed, many of whom were zealous for the law (see Acts 21:20). Gradually, many of these converted priests brought their legalism right into the young church in Jerusalem. Towards the end of the book of Acts the apostle Paul was prevailed upon to shave his head, take a vow and go into the temple. Legalism spelled trouble for Paul, and he fought a running battle with this loathsome blight that had found its way in where it did not belong.

Paul's letter to the Galatians handles the matter very fully. Paul had planted a pure church in Galatia through his gospel preaching. Later he was stunned to learn that legalism was creeping in, so he wrote to them, 'Did you suffer so many things in vain?' (Gal 3:4). You could ask the same of those with Nehemiah—'You worked so hard to restore the city. Did you suffer so many things in vain? You have invited Tobiah right back in!' Paul was horrified that the Galatians had freshly embraced the law.

> At that time, when you did not know God, you were slaves to those which by nature are no gods. But now that you have come to know God, how is it that you turn back again to the weak and worthless elemental things, to which you desire to be enslaved all over again? You observe days and months and seasons and years. I fear for you, that perhaps I have labored over you in vain (Gal 4:8–11).

The gospel had brought them into freedom. Was it all in vain? Had they subjected themselves again to the same bondage? A few lines later, Paul asked:

> Tell me, you who want to be under law, are you not aware of what the law says? For it is written that Abraham had two sons, one by the slave woman and the other by the free woman. His son by the slave woman was born in the ordinary way; but his son by the free woman was born as the result of a promise.
>
> These things may be taken figuratively, for the women represent two covenants. One covenant is from Mount Sinai and bears children who are to be slaves: This is Hagar. Now Hagar stands for Mount Sinai in Arabia and corresponds to the present city of Jerusalem, because she is in slavery with her children. But the Jerusalem that is above is free, and she is our mother...
>
> Now you, brothers, like Isaac, are children of promise. At that time the son born in the ordinary way persecuted the son born by the power of the Spirit. It is the same now. But what does the Scripture say? "Get rid of the slave woman and her son, for the slave woman's son will never share in the inheritance with the free woman's son." Therefore, brothers, we are not children of the slave woman, but of the free woman.
>
> It is for freedom that Christ has set us free. Stand firm, then, and do not let yourselves be burdened again by a yoke of slavery (Gal 4:21—5:1, NIV).

How similar to the situation faced by Nehemiah! A church which was pure, the product of the gospel, had once again embraced legalism—that product of human endeavour with all its rules and regulations, observing certain rules, wearing certain clothes, endeavouring to obey certain laws. Nehemiah's answer to Tobiah was to say, 'Throw him out and all his furniture with him!' Paul's answer to the law was, 'Cast out the bond woman and her son.'

We are born again that we might reign in life, not through laws which we impose upon ourselves, for the law will always condemn us (as Romans 7 makes perfectly plain). If we seek sanctification through observance of the law, we will ultimately meet with frustration and condemnation. The law cannot sanctify us. God gave us the law to lead us to Christ. Christ is the end of the law to everyone who believes (Rom 10:4). We are discharged from the law (Rom 7:6) and, although the law will never pass away, Christians can rejoice that they have died to the law through the body of Christ!

### A new husband!

There is no way into joy, freedom and peace of mind by being married to the law. The law is totally impotent. As Paul argues in Galatians 3: 'If a law had been given which was able to *impart life*, then righteousness would have indeed been based on the law' (v.21). But the law cannot impart life. The law can point out our faults and show us where we are going wrong, but it does not give life. It only leads to condemnation.

When we are saved, Jesus invites us to come to him. He unites us with him in his death to the law. We are also united to him in resurrection life and have now become his Bride. Whereas our old husband, the law, merely told us what to do but never gave us life or help, Jesus says, 'Abide in Me, and I in you, and you will bear much fruit' (see Matthew 15:4). Jesus is a life-imparting husband! He can plant his seed in me and bring forth fruit. So, I grow up in Christ not by returning to law but by developing my relationship with Jesus.

Nehemiah was outraged—'How did Tobiah get back into the temple?' Paul was outraged—'Cast out the bond woman and her child!' Today we must cast out legalism— have nothing to do with it. Instead, learn to live in close fellowship with the Lord Jesus and have his living words in you. His words are Spirit and life. Feed on them. He is the Bread of Life. He is food for your soul. His word brings forth faith. Get to know Jesus, love him and obey him. Do these things and you will be fruitful. For the letter kills but the Spirit gives life!

# 23

## *Till the Day Dawns*

Another disappointment for Nehemiah on his return to Jerusalem was that the people had not continued to tithe faithfully in support of the Levites. 'The portions of the Levites had not been given them, so that the Levites and the singers who performed the service had gone away, each to his own field' (Neh 13:10–12). They had begun to lose their corporate vision and had stopped giving. Originally, as pioneers, they had left their homes in Babylon and risked everything. Returning to Jerusalem had cost them dearly. Nevertheless, they had begun well in their commitment to tithing to the Levites. Gradually, they began to settle. Now the walls were up, they were secure, and the people's commitment had run dry so that the Levites had to resort to working on their fields.

Originally, God had not planned for them to have any land. The eleven tribes had territory of their own and gave a tenth of their income to keep the Levites, but now this God-ordained means of support had evaporated.

Our financial giving often reflects our whole-heartedness. It authenticates our devotion to Christ and his church. Where our treasure is, there our heart is also. It has been said that Christianity is the most secular religion in the world. In other words, the Bible says more about hard cash than any other religious book. Other religious books trade in philosophies and abstract thoughts, whereas the Bible speaks to real people in a real twentieth century, making it plain that if we cannot honour God with our giving there is something wrong with our faith, love and sense of commitment.

We must not only be generous givers but also committed, regular givers to our local church. Our chief responsibility in giving is to home base. If we have made sure we have fulfilled our responsibilities there, we are also free to give further afield. But if we have godly leadership, why not trust them to channel resources around the world? Your part is to show your faithfulness to your local work by systematically giving there.

It has to be asked whether ministers are receiving a proper wage. Through the system of tithing, the Levites received just above the average of the income of the other tribes. It could be argued, therefore, that a minister should earn something consistent with the average salary in his congregation, with a little more for the extra expenses he incurs. Some churches argue that they only give a small salary but they do provide a house. In other words, the man has a tied house with all the insecurity that that brings and which he loses at retirement and can never call his own. We need to look into this. It is very difficult for ministers to preach about giving because of the obvious implications, and they can be accused of feathering their own nest. It is a simple matter for them to preach about justification by faith or evangelism or holiness—but it is not easy for them to take the theme of giving in their pulpit. Perhaps you are one of those who have the responsibility of deciding your minister's salary. Let me encourage you to look realistically and, if necessary, radically at the whole subject and care properly for the man that God has put among you to serve you in the word. As Paul said to the Corinthians, 'Just as you excel in everything... excel in this grace of giving' (2 Cor 8:7, NIV).

**Being different**

The third area that Nehemiah encountered on his return was the people's departure from keeping the sabbath. The people were treading out the wine presses, bringing in sacks of grain, loading them on donkeys—and all this on the sabbath day. Sabbath observance was one of those features that made the Israelites distinctive from all the other nations. Other nations worked and bought and sold on the sabbath, but Israel was to be different in this particular way. They were not to be involved in any of these routine activities from Friday evening, when they began to celebrate the sabbath, right through to Saturday night.

Merchants and traders from other nations expected 'business as usual' seven days a week, and in Nehemiah's absence, the Jews had gradually conceded to their style. The sabbath day in Jerusalem had become like any other day.

Nehemiah immediately rebuked them and ordered the doors to be shut. When some tradesmen actually camped outside the city, Nehemiah threatened to lay hands on them, and placed guards on the gates.

We must, of course, understand that the sabbath was something which was instituted for the Jewish nation. Colossians 2:16–17 says, 'Let no one act as your judge in regard to food or drink or in respect to a festival or a new moon or a Sabbath day—things which are a mere shadow of what is to come; but the substance belongs to Christ.' Or as Paul argues: 'One man regards one day above another, another regards every day alike' (Rom 14:5). Paul's conclusion is that each one should be fully convinced in his own mind. It is evident, then, that the New Testament does not regard sabbath-keeping as a vital theme in the way that it obviously was in the Old Testament era.

The enduring fact is that the people of God are meant

to be different! We are to be 'blameless and innocent, children of God above reproach in the midst of a crooked and perverse generation, among whom you appear as lights in the world' (Phil 2:15). We are to 'keep [our] behaviour excellent among the Gentiles' (1 Pet 2:12). Peter goes on to argue, 'For the time already past is sufficient for you to have carried out the desire of the Gentiles...they are surprised that you do not run with them' (1 Pet 4:3–4). Are they surprised? Do you cause surprises at work and at home? Peter says that is one of the marks of the Christian—he causes his colleagues to be surprised! You used to be heavily involved, but now you have changed. That time past was sufficient. God expects the Christian to live a completely different lifestyle.

### Grace to say 'no'

We must not consider the grace of God to mean 'easy believism'. God's grace is not meant to be blurring the edge of our commitment to holy living. In fact, Paul reminds us in Titus 2 that 'the grace of God...has appeared...It teaches us to say "no" to ungodliness...and to live self-controlled, upright and godly lives in this present age' (vv.11–12, NIV). The rest of the world may be bent on destruction, but the grace of God teaches us to say 'no'. We are called upstream against the flow. In our generation, young people will often be called to demonstrate the grace of God by saying 'no'.

Originally these Jews had been so zealous to build the walls, so keen to march around them celebrating the distinctiveness that they represented, yet all that labour to build the walls had become futile because they now allowed unrighteousness to come through the gates. Like Joseph, we are to be steadfast in refusing evil.

In Nehemiah's absence the returned exiles had become so careless about retaining their distinctiveness that their children no longer knew how to speak the language of

Judah, but were beginning to speak the language of the other peoples (Neh 13:24). They had even given their daughters in marriage to the other nations. How painful this must have been for Nehemiah. His original burden was to build the walls. His heart ached that the people of God should be distinctive and different. He fought against every obstacle and laboured night and day to erect the walls, only to find the next generation carelessly going through the gates and committing themselves even to the marriage bond with the ungodly. What fellowship has light with darkness? How can believers be bound together with unbelievers? At a superficial level believers can find common ground with unbelievers. They can enjoy the same music, similar books, an interest in sport; but these superficial distractions are not the rock on which to build a home—they are the very sand which causes final heart-break and collapse.

To say that Nehemiah dealt with it ruthlessly is to understate the case. As a true reformer, his zeal knew no limits!

### It's all over!

Finally, I would like to point out the way in which the book ends. Chapter 13 tells us all about the ongoing battles which will be there till the end. Then, strangely, we read what seem very mundane words: 'I arranged for the supply of wood at appointed times and for the first fruits. Remember me, O my God, for good.' And suddenly, the book is finished. It does not even say that they lived happily ever after! It suddenly stops. As I contemplated this strange conclusion I asked the Lord what it meant. I felt that God told me that it reminds us that we are moving swiftly to a moment when everything will suddenly end. We shall all be working, as they were at the end of the book of Acts which stops in a similar way. The book of Acts is not concluded with a flourish, recording that thousands were being swept into the kingdom in Rome. It simply says: 'And [Paul] stayed two full years in his own rented quarters...preaching the kingdom of God.'

One day the world is simply going to stop. It will not necessarily be on the last night of a tremendous international convention. The word will not sweep around the nations. Large conferences will not be organized with huge choirs to prepare for the end. It will be like the end of the book of Nehemiah, who was making provision for contributions of wood. Suddenly everything is finished. You might say, 'I thought there was some more.' No more! Finished! It will suddenly all be over. The Bible is very plain that this is how it will be—like a thief in the night. In the days of Noah they were marrying, buying, selling, working—suddenly, that was it! We are near to that day. No more church history. No more world. No more of this fleeting time. The end of this present age. Gone!

# Restoration in the Church

## by Terry Virgo

God is restoring his church. Many are now seeing the need to apply New Testament principles to their church structures and time-honoured traditions. Flexibility and freedom are on the increase.

This book takes an inside look at what has been called 'the house church movement' and reveals how amazing growth has come from a rediscovery of Scripture's teaching on ministries in the church. Whatever our situation, we will find a fresh challenge in what the author has to say.

☐ The traditional evangelical is reminded that restoration is rooted in the orthodox teaching of the Reformers.

☐ The charismatic is asked not to stop with personal gifts but to go on to embrace the ministries of apostle and prophet.

☐ Those already committed to restoration are urged to be watchful, avoiding complacency and ready to move on to whatever God has in store.

Terry Virgo is based at Clarendon Church, Hove, Brighton. A frequent visitor to many countries with the message of restoration, he is highly respected for his ministry to church leaders in various denominations, and is a popular speaker at Bible Weeks each year. He is married with five children.

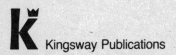

Kingsway Publications

# Weak People, Mighty God

## By Terry Virgo

Often we can learn more about God through reading stories than by studying concepts. Whereas we sometimes struggle with a principle, we can very quickly identify with a person.

David, Elijah and Jonah were three ordinary people. They did not set out to be heroes of the faith. Nor were they always ready to let God move in their lives. But he did, and as a result they were transformed.

If you are conscious of your own limitations, your fallibility, you have a choice. You can give up and resign yourself to a lifetime of ineffectiveness - or you can learn from people like David, Elijah and Jonah, who discovered that it is the weak in whom God chooses to display his strength and reveal his glory.

This book is an invitation to respond to the grace of a God who will never fail you or forsake you.

TERRY VIRGO is based at Clarendon Church, Brighton, where he leads New Frontiers International, a ministry dedicated to building up the lives of Christian men and women in many lands.

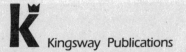

Kingsway Publications